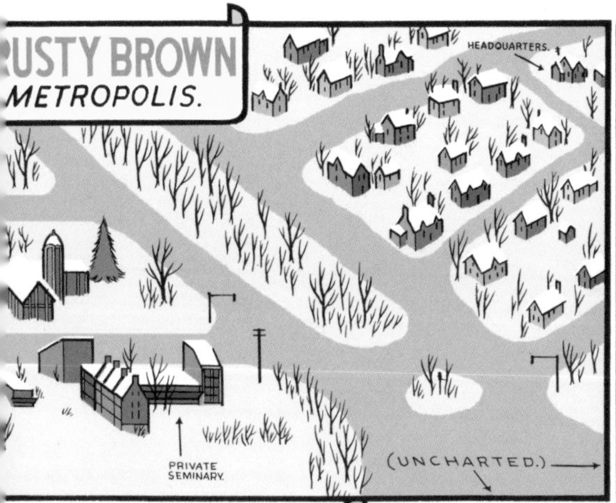
RUSTY BROWN
METROPOLIS.
HEADQUARTERS.
PRIVATE SEMINARY.
(UNCHARTED.)

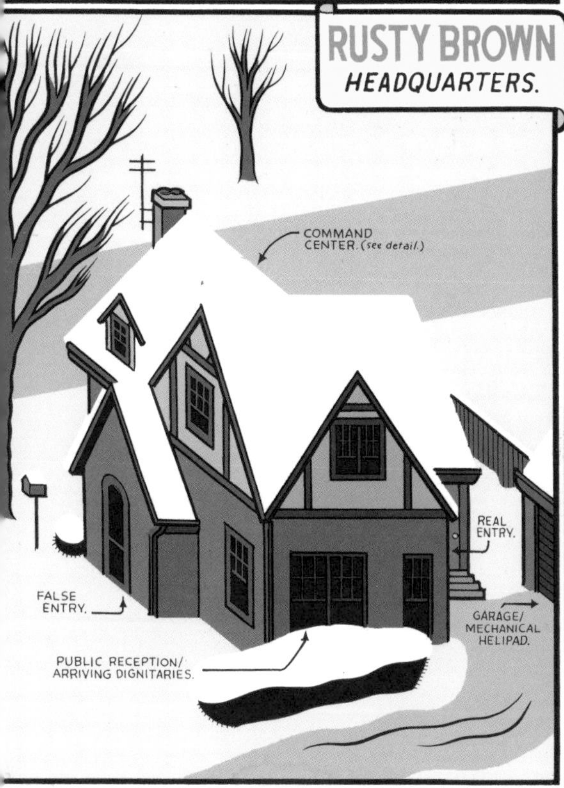
RUSTY BROWN
HEADQUARTERS.
COMMAND CENTER. (see detail.)
REAL ENTRY.
FALSE ENTRY.
GARAGE/ MECHANICAL HELIPAD.
PUBLIC RECEPTION/ ARRIVING DIGNITARIES.

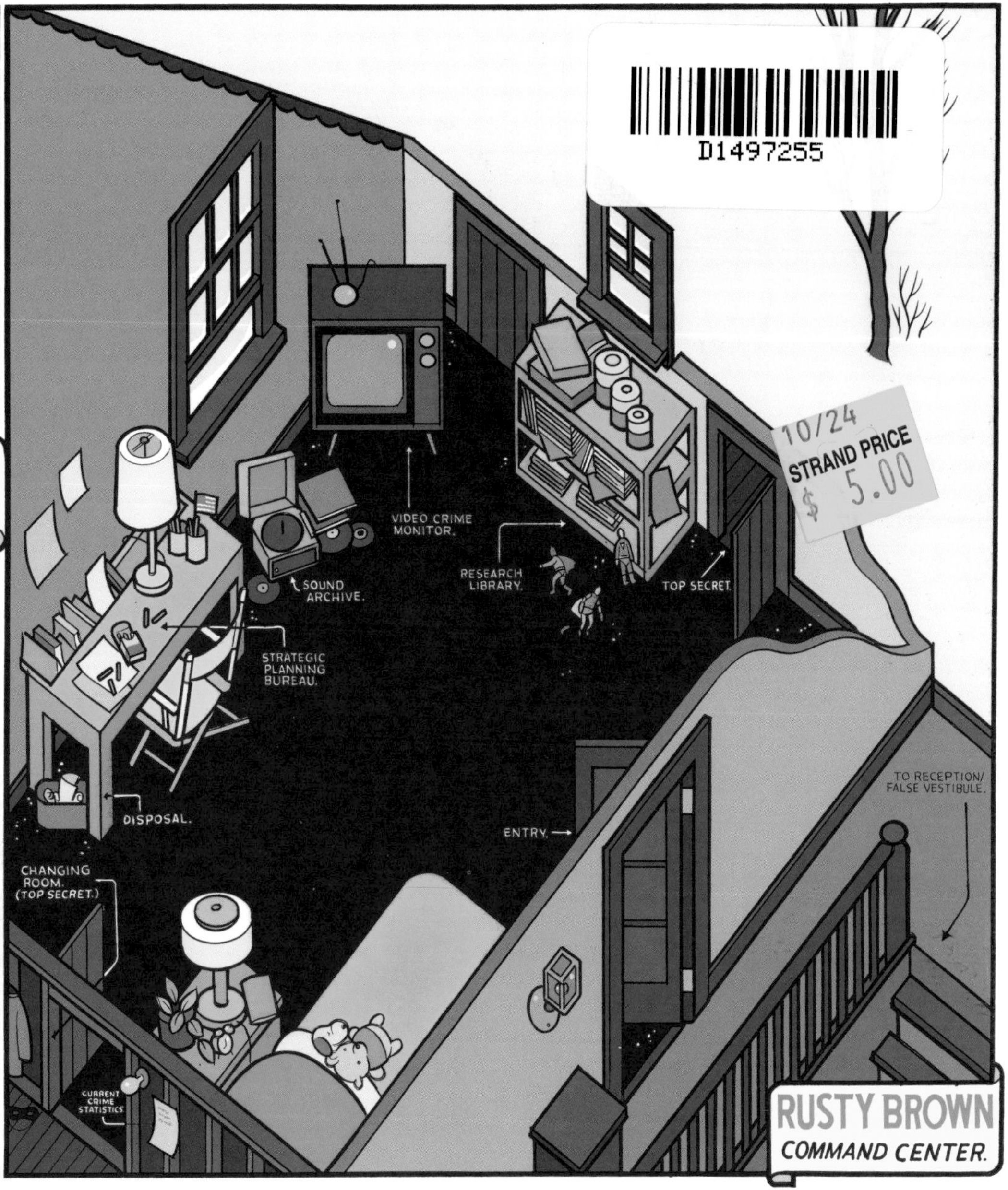
VIDEO CRIME MONITOR.
SOUND ARCHIVE.
RESEARCH LIBRARY.
TOP SECRET.
STRATEGIC PLANNING BUREAU.
DISPOSAL.
ENTRY.
CHANGING ROOM. (TOP SECRET.)
TO RECEPTION/ FALSE VESTIBULE.
CURRENT CRIME STATISTICS
RUSTY BROWN
COMMAND CENTER.

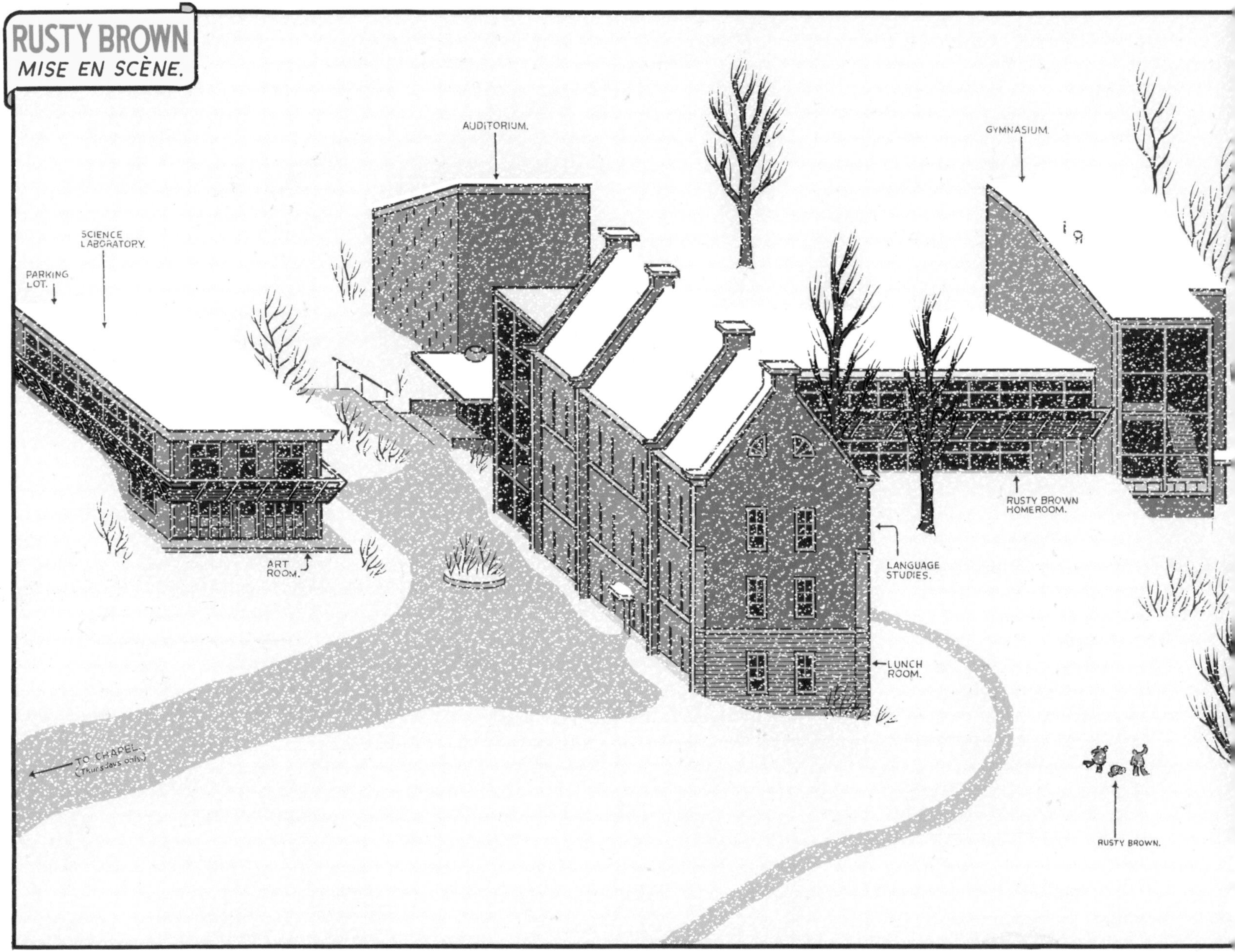
RUSTY BROWN
MISE EN SCÈNE.
AUDITORIUM.
GYMNASIUM.
SCIENCE LABORATORY.
PARKING LOT.
ART ROOM.
RUSTY BROWN HOMEROOM.
LANGUAGE STUDIES.
LUNCH ROOM.
TO CHAPEL (Thursdays only)
RUSTY BROWN.

"No two are alike,"
any schoolchild will tell you.

And indeed, of the few thousand snowflakes
captured on paper or film since man began
studying them roughly three centuries ago,
no true matches have been found.

But what of the billion trillion or so
that haven't been seen — or, more properly, won't *ever* be seen?
Isn't it possible that at least two of them
might be *somewhat* similar?

In 1655, the scientist Robert Hooke first tried to sketch
what René Descartes had described as the "little roses" or
"wheels with six teeth" that collected around him
in mounds and drifts.

Peering as closely as he could with one of the world's first microscopes, Hooke's subjects nonetheless melted away as he drew them, his pictures more the product of memory than of direct observation. Fortunately, however, with the precise photographic techniques available to us today, scientists are now able to "stop in time" the natural evaporation of snowflakes so that we all may study their beauty for as long as we like.

While a snowflake on a finger lingers only a second before resolving back into a drop of water, freezing that drop of water will not produce a snowflake — it will only produce a little bead of ice.

The exquisite, miraculous shape of a snowflake is a result of the singular path it takes through utterly unique conditions of cloudiness, temperature, and humidity, a veritable picture of its whole life from its birth as a speck of dirt to its end as a fragile miniature crystal flower.

Like the growing rings of a tiny hexagonal tree, billions of water molecules spin around and around, each finding the closest, easiest, and most comfortable bond (just as people, who seek the companionship of like minds and bodies, cannot simply be thrown together and expect to thrive) until, with no room left to fall, the whole finds its way to your snowshovel, glove, or

TSSHHT

RUSTY

BROWN

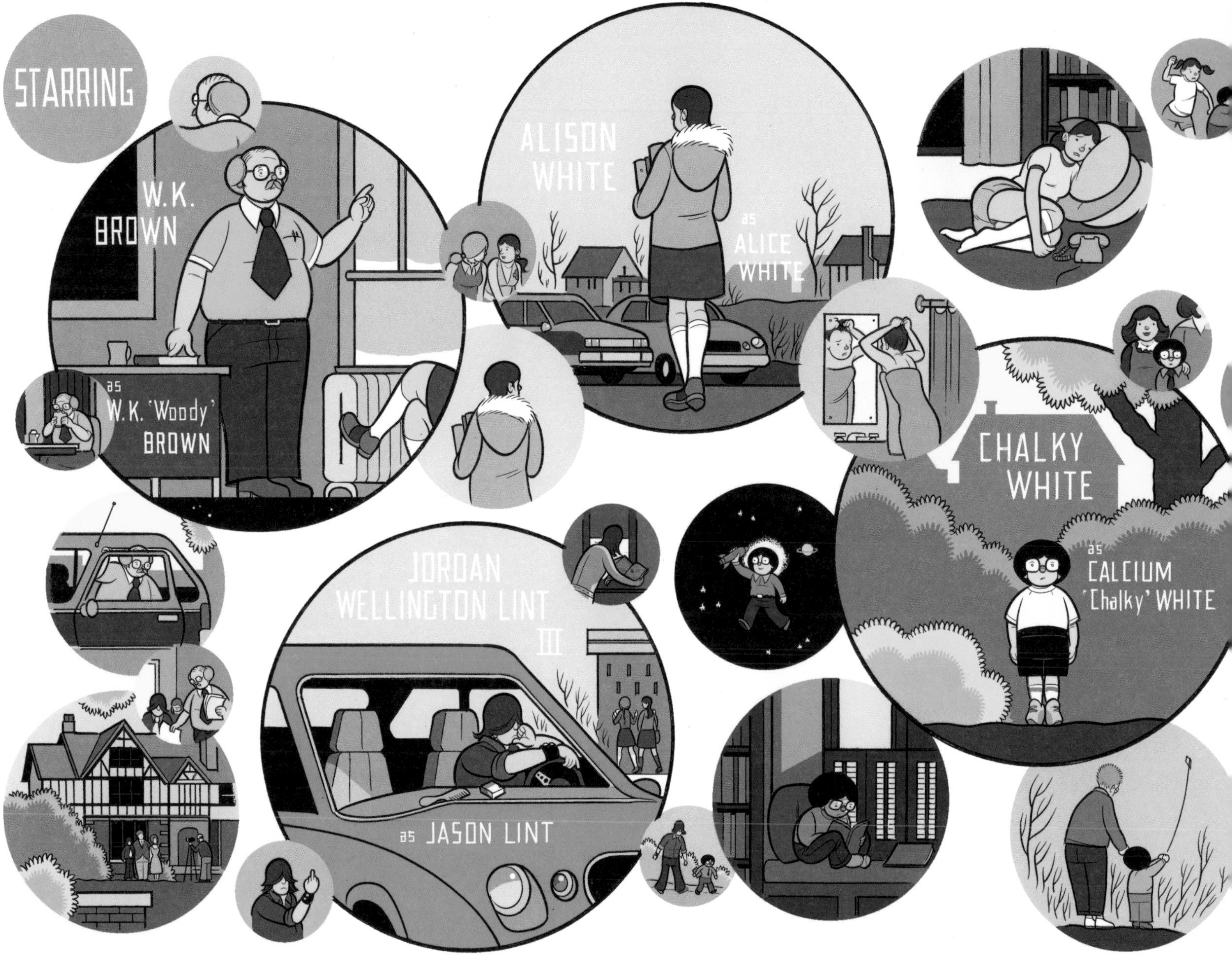
STARRING
W.K. BROWN
as W.K. 'Woody' BROWN
ALISON WHITE
as ALICE WHITE
CHALKY WHITE
as CALCIUM 'Chalky' WHITE
JORDAN WELLINGTON LINT III
as JASON LINT

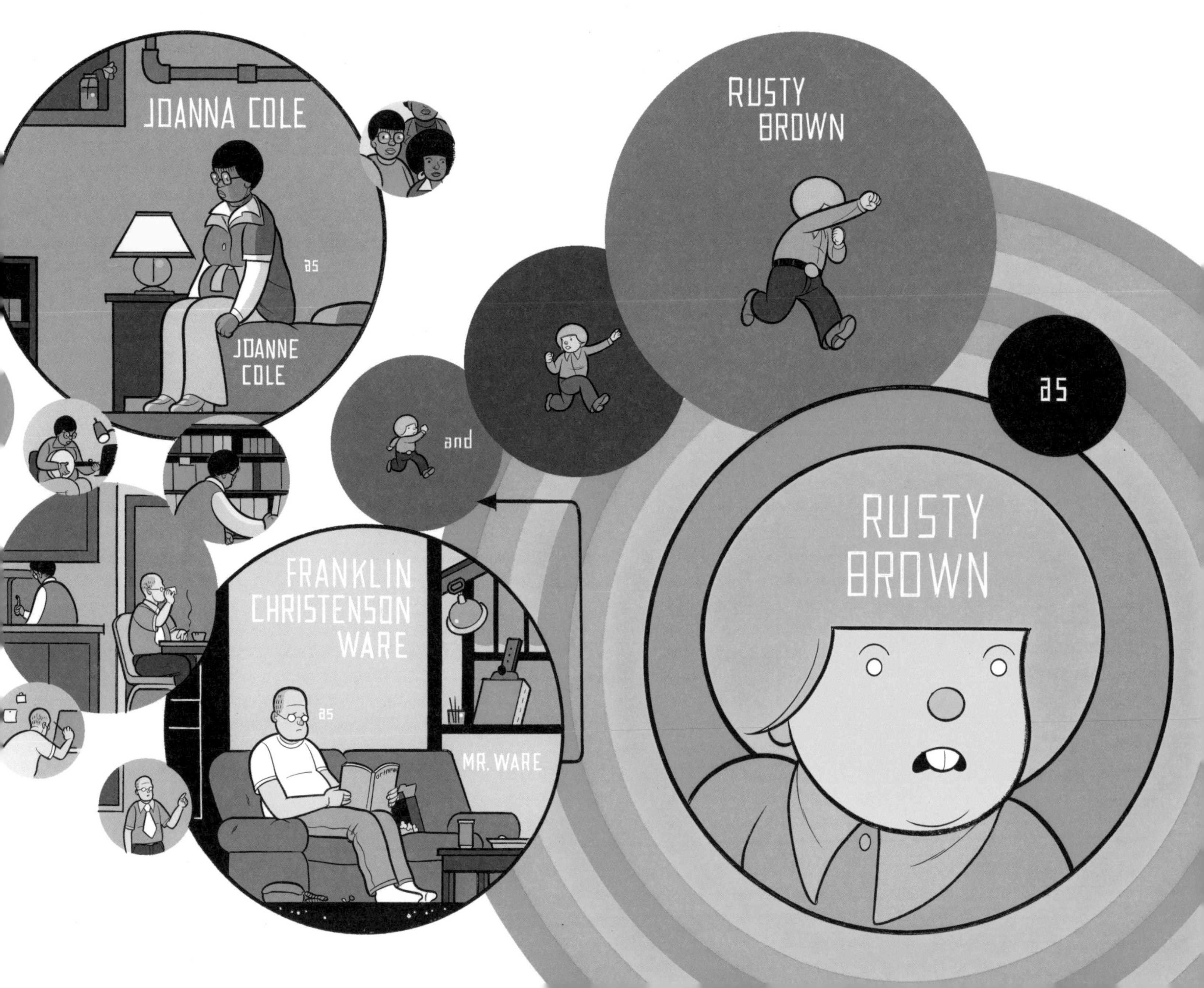

JOANNA COLE
as
JOANNE COLE
and
RUSTY BROWN
as
RUSTY BROWN
FRANKLIN CHRISTENSON WARE
as
MR. WARE

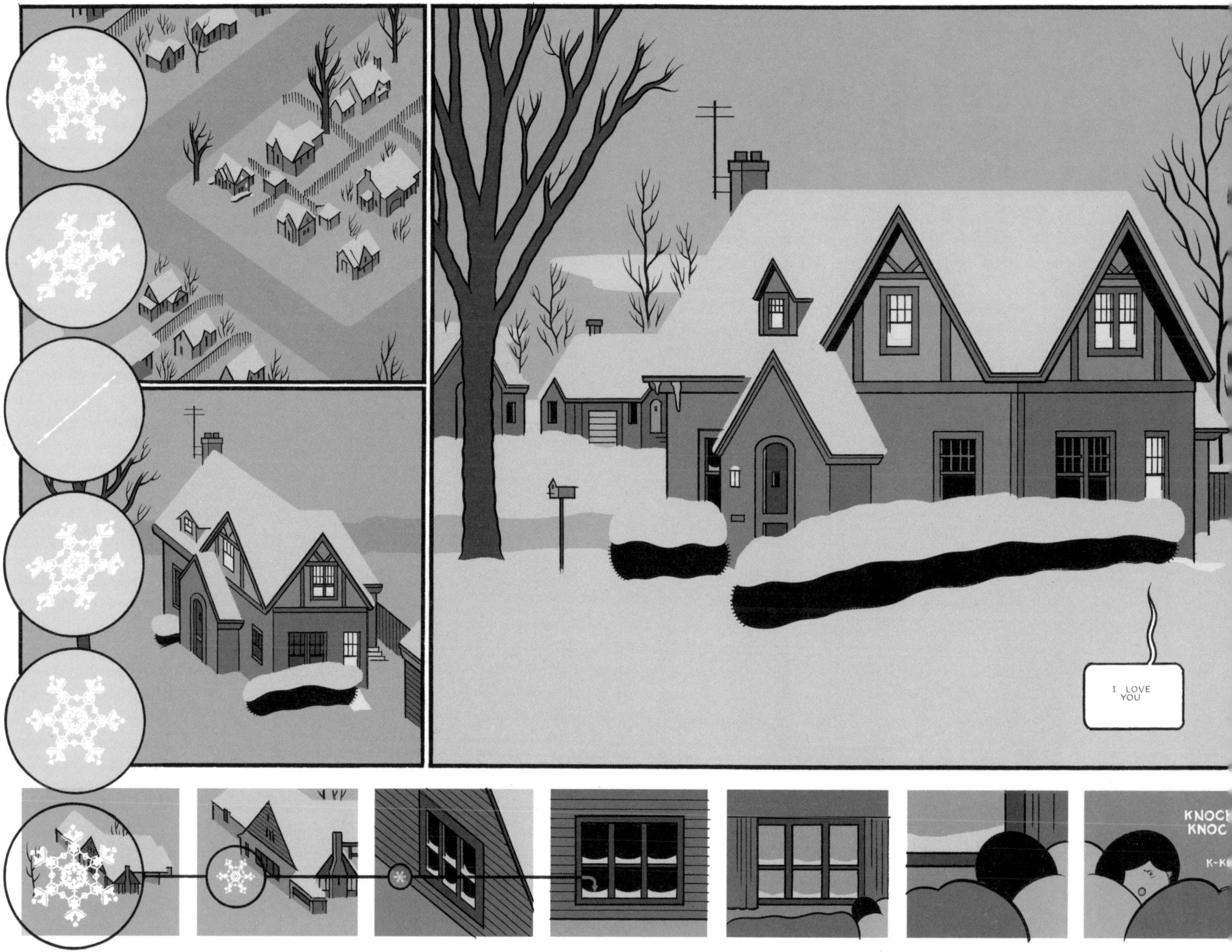
I LOVE YOU

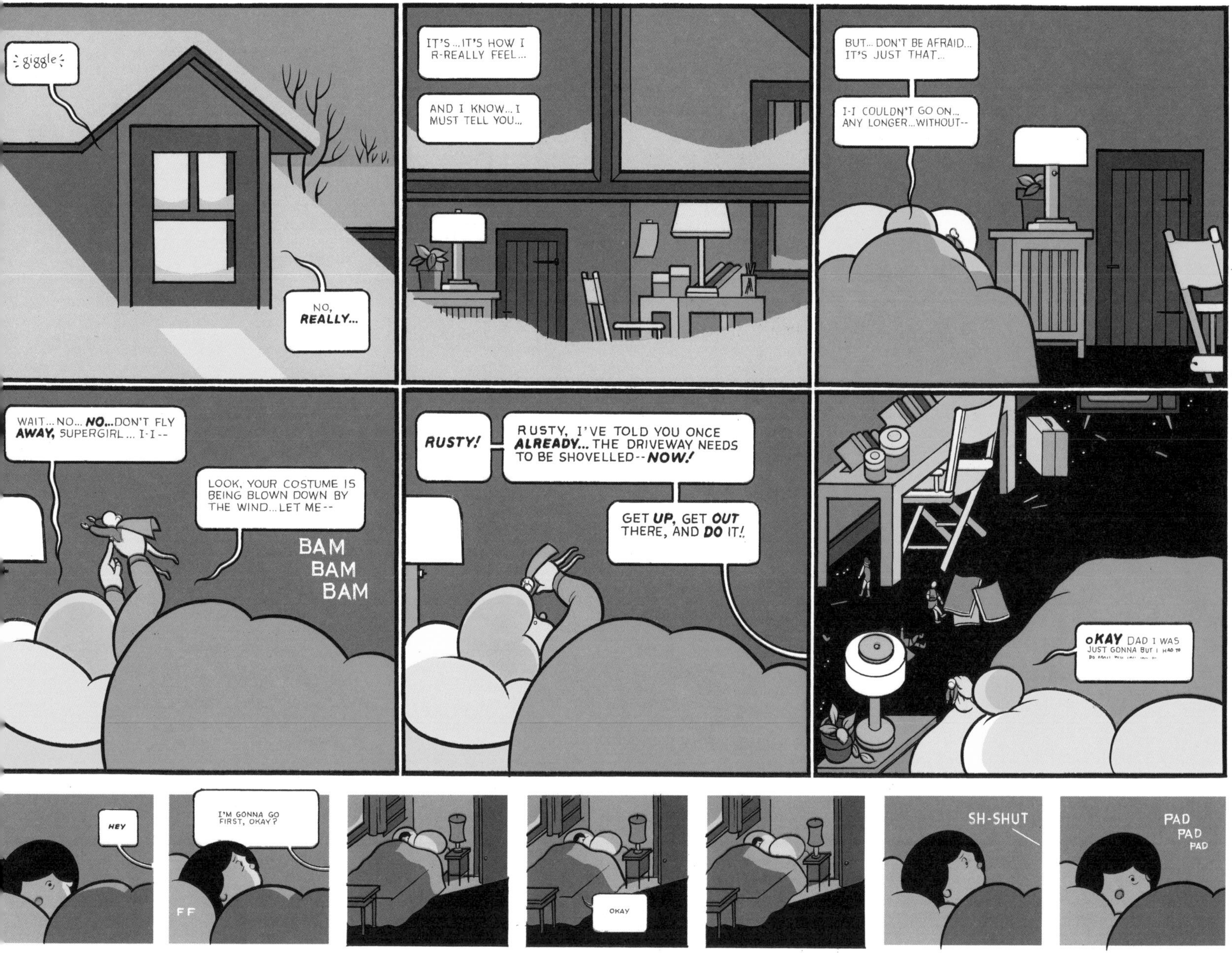
giggle
NO, REALLY...
IT'S... IT'S HOW I R-REALLY FEEL...
AND I KNOW... I MUST TELL YOU...
BUT... DON'T BE AFRAID... IT'S JUST THAT...
I-I COULDN'T GO ON... ANY LONGER... WITHOUT--
WAIT... NO... NO... DON'T FLY AWAY, SUPERGIRL... I-I--
LOOK, YOUR COSTUME IS BEING BLOWN DOWN BY THE WIND... LET ME--
BAM
BAM
BAM
RUSTY!
RUSTY, I'VE TOLD YOU ONCE ALREADY... THE DRIVEWAY NEEDS TO BE SHOVELLED--NOW!
GET UP, GET OUT THERE, AND DO IT!
OKAY DAD I WAS JUST GONNA BUT I HAD TO
HEY
I'M GONNA GO FIRST, OKAY?
FF
OKAY
SH-SHUT
PAD
PAD
PAD

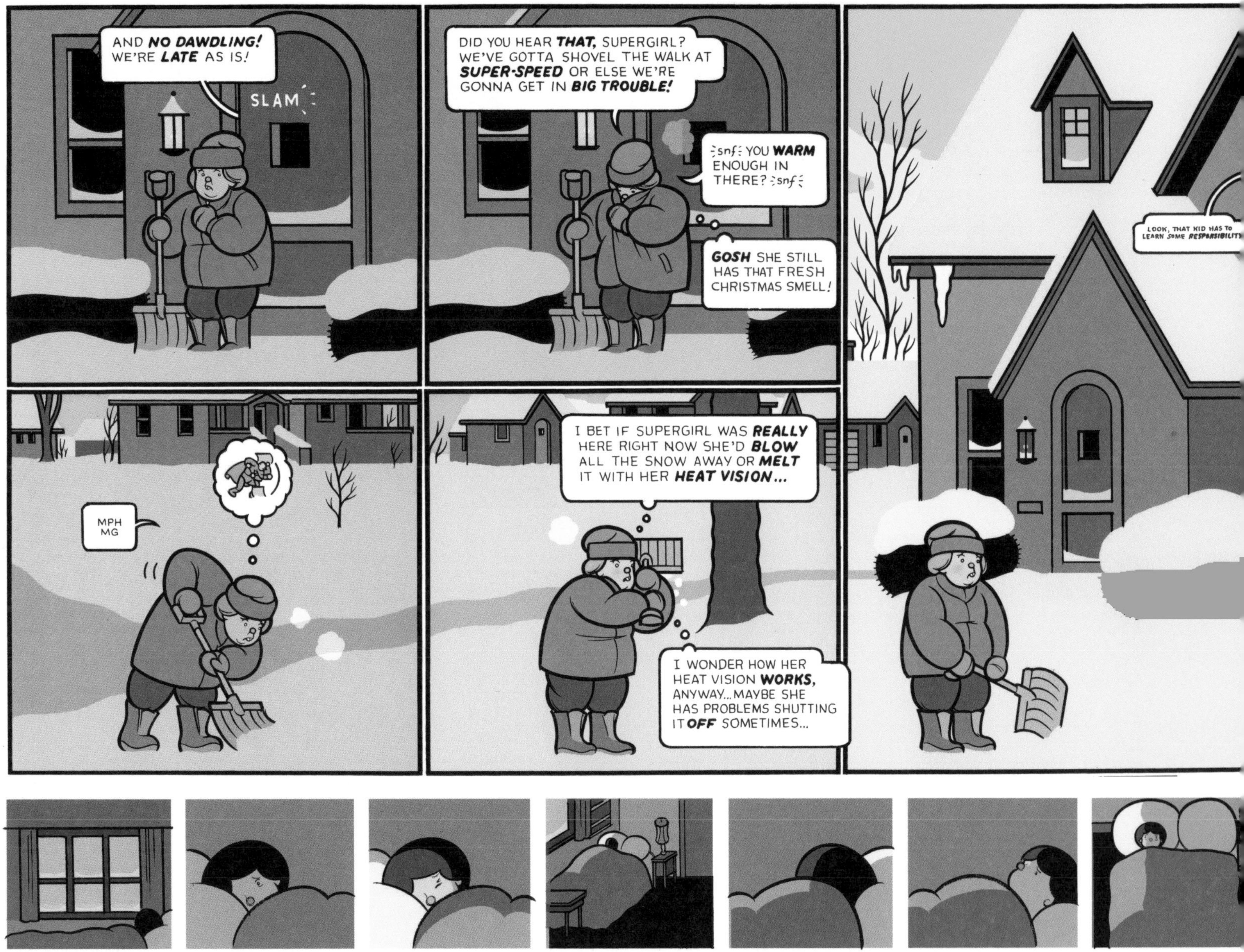
AND NO DAWDLING! WE'RE LATE AS IS!
SLAM
DID YOU HEAR THAT, SUPERGIRL? WE'VE GOTTA SHOVEL THE WALK AT SUPER-SPEED OR ELSE WE'RE GONNA GET IN BIG TROUBLE!
snf YOU WARM ENOUGH IN THERE? snf
GOSH SHE STILL HAS THAT FRESH CHRISTMAS SMELL!
MPH MG
I BET IF SUPERGIRL WAS REALLY HERE RIGHT NOW SHE'D BLOW ALL THE SNOW AWAY OR MELT IT WITH HER HEAT VISION...
I WONDER HOW HER HEAT VISION WORKS, ANYWAY... MAYBE SHE HAS PROBLEMS SHUTTING IT OFF SOMETIMES...
LOOK, THAT KID HAS TO LEARN SOME RESPONSIBILITY

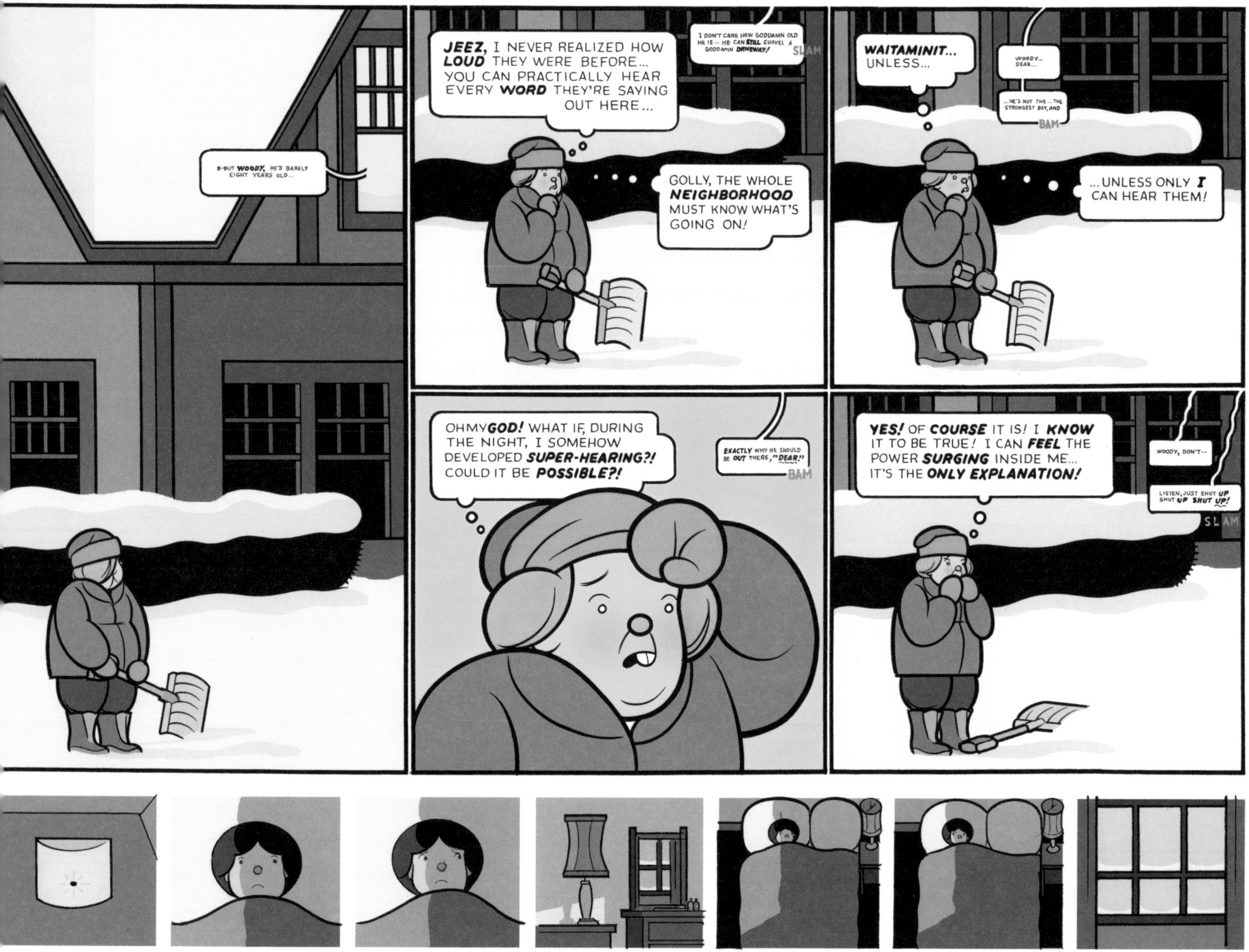
B-BUT WOODY, HE'S BARELY EIGHT YEARS OLD...
JEEZ, I NEVER REALIZED HOW LOUD THEY WERE BEFORE... YOU CAN PRACTICALLY HEAR EVERY WORD THEY'RE SAYING OUT HERE...
I DON'T CARE HOW GODDAMN OLD HE IS -- HE CAN STILL SHOVEL A GODDAMN DRIVEWAY!
SLAM
GOLLY, THE WHOLE NEIGHBORHOOD MUST KNOW WHAT'S GOING ON!
WAITAMINIT... UNLESS...
WOODY... DEAR...
...HE'S NOT THE... THE STRONGEST BOY, AND
BAM
...UNLESS ONLY I CAN HEAR THEM!
OHMYGOD! WHAT IF, DURING THE NIGHT, I SOMEHOW DEVELOPED SUPER-HEARING?! COULD IT BE POSSIBLE?!
EXACTLY WHY HE SHOULD BE OUT THERE, "DEAR."
BAM
YES! OF COURSE IT IS! I KNOW IT TO BE TRUE! I CAN FEEL THE POWER SURGING INSIDE ME... IT'S THE ONLY EXPLANATION!
WOODY, DON'T--
LISTEN, JUST SHUT UP SHUT UP SHUT UP!
SLAM

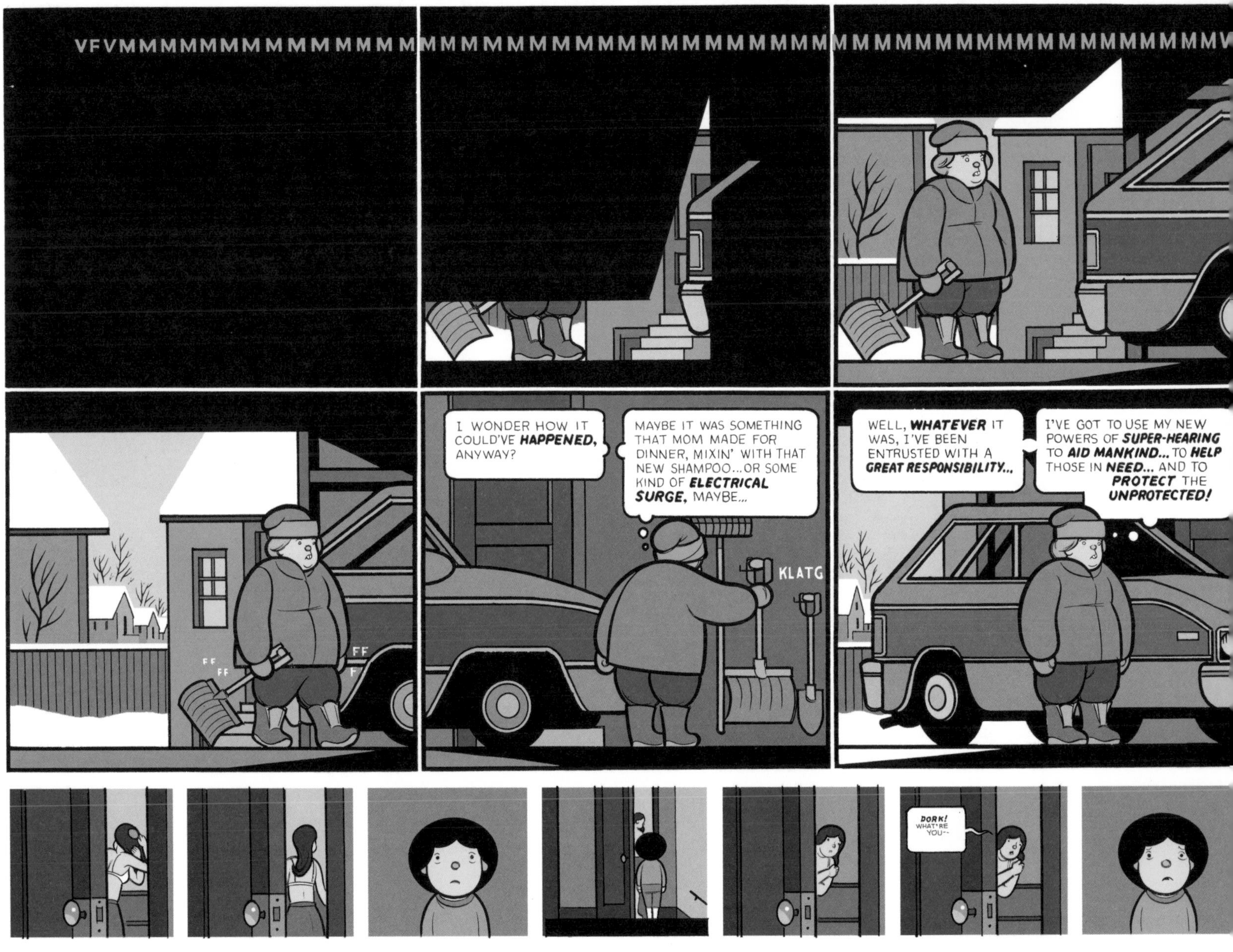
VFVMMMMMMMMMMMMMMMMMMMMMMMMMMMMMMMMMMMMMMMMMMMMMMMMMMMV
FF FF
FF F
I WONDER HOW IT COULD'VE **HAPPENED,** ANYWAY?
MAYBE IT WAS SOMETHING THAT MOM MADE FOR DINNER, MIXIN' WITH THAT NEW SHAMPOO...OR SOME KIND OF **ELECTRICAL SURGE,** MAYBE...
KLATG
WELL, **WHATEVER** IT WAS, I'VE BEEN ENTRUSTED WITH A **GREAT RESPONSIBILITY...**
I'VE GOT TO USE MY NEW POWERS OF **SUPER-HEARING** TO **AID MANKIND...** TO **HELP** THOSE IN **NEED...** AND TO **PROTECT** THE **UNPROTECTED!**
DORK! WHAT'RE YOU--

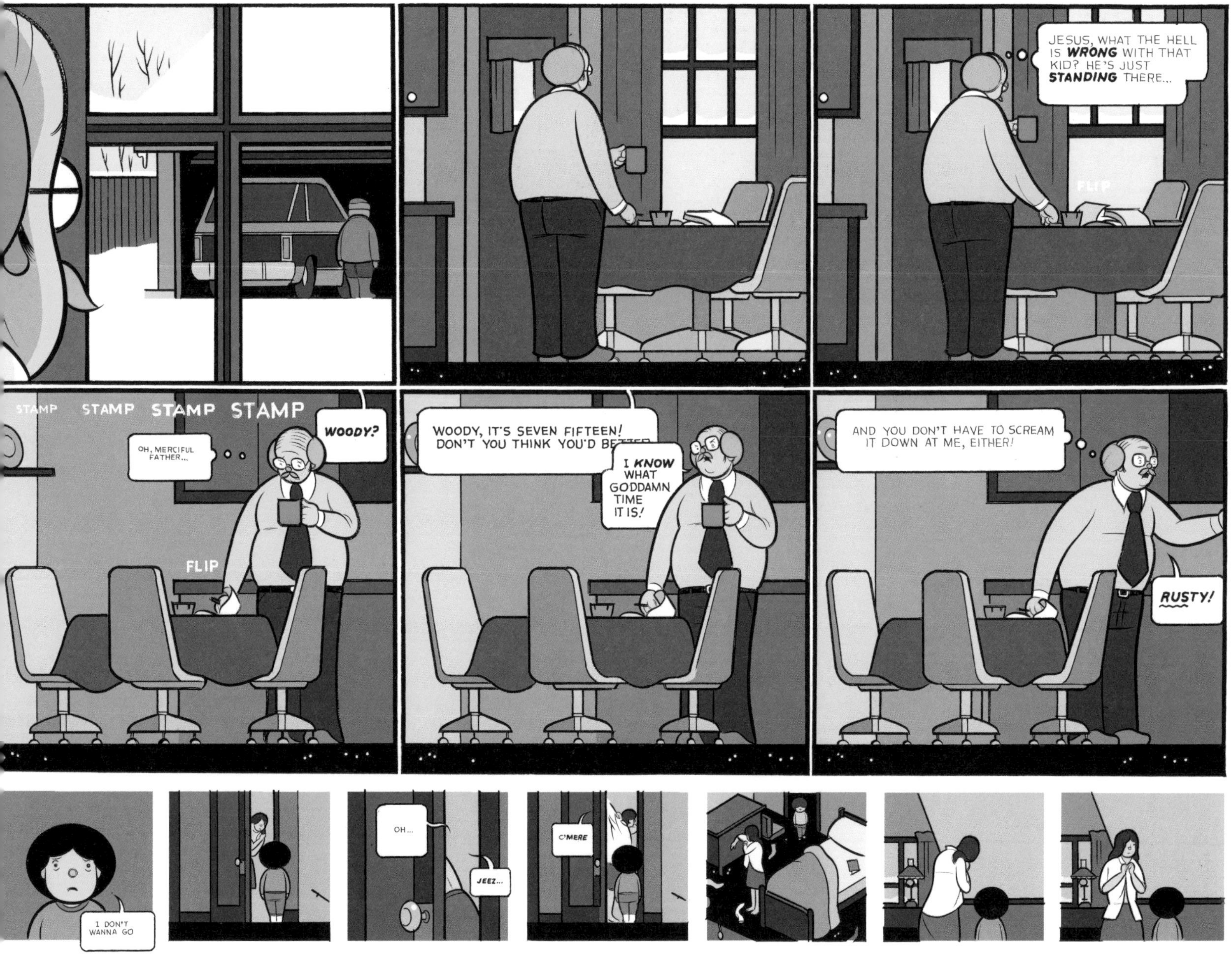
JESUS, WHAT THE HELL IS WRONG WITH THAT KID? HE'S JUST STANDING THERE...
FLIP
STAMP STAMP STAMP STAMP
OH, MERCIFUL FATHER...
WOODY?
FLIP
WOODY, IT'S SEVEN FIFTEEN! DON'T YOU THINK YOU'D BE
I KNOW WHAT GODDAMN TIME IT IS!
AND YOU DON'T HAVE TO SCREAM IT DOWN AT ME, EITHER!
RUSTY!
I DON'T WANNA GO
OH...
JEEZ...
C'MERE

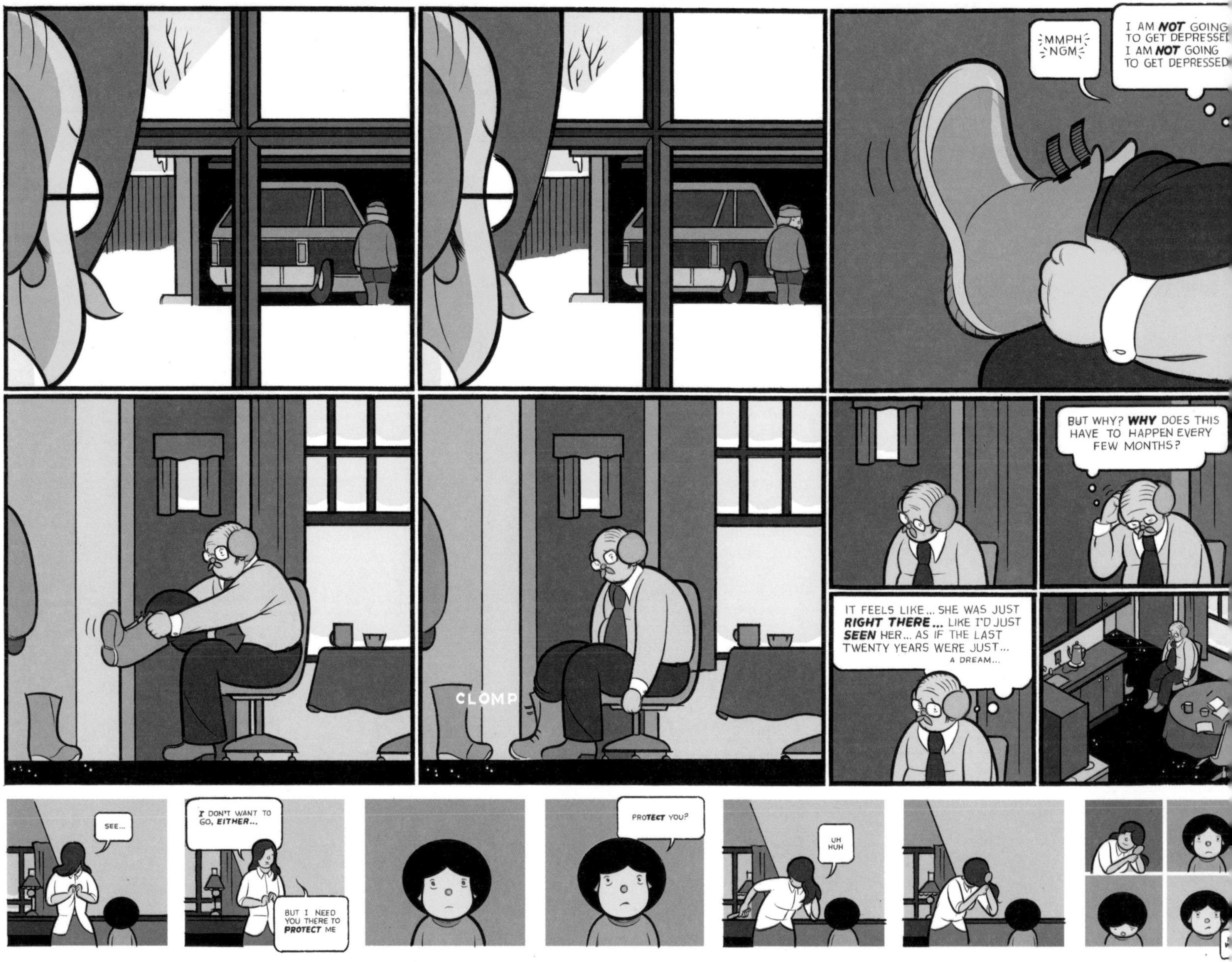
MMPH NGM
I AM NOT GOING TO GET DEPRESSED
I AM NOT GOING TO GET DEPRESSED
CLOMP
BUT WHY? WHY DOES THIS HAVE TO HAPPEN EVERY FEW MONTHS?
IT FEELS LIKE... SHE WAS JUST RIGHT THERE... LIKE I'D JUST SEEN HER... AS IF THE LAST TWENTY YEARS WERE JUST... A DREAM...
SEE...
I DON'T WANT TO GO, EITHER...
BUT I NEED YOU THERE TO PROTECT ME
PROTECT YOU?
UH HUH

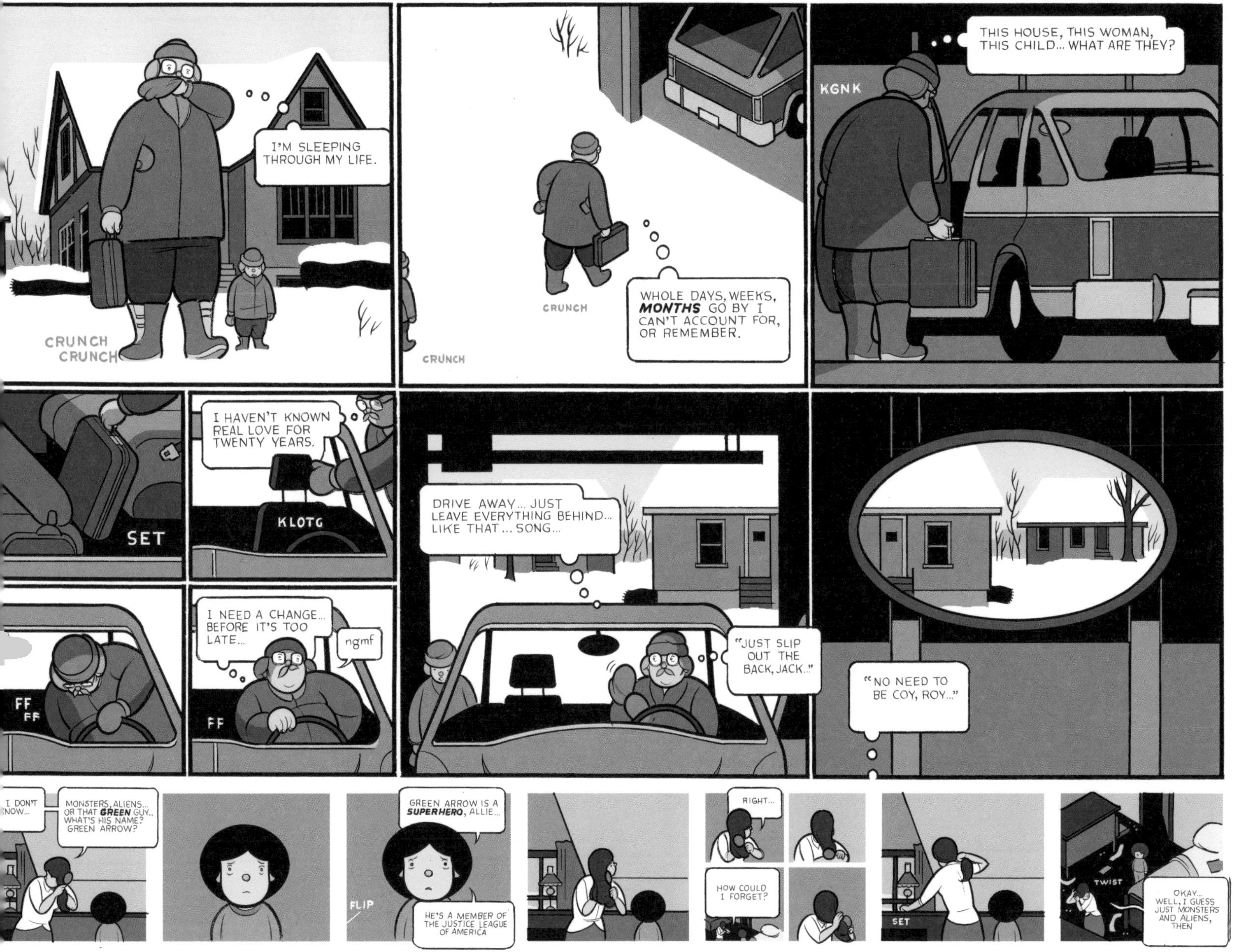
I'M SLEEPING THROUGH MY LIFE.
CRUNCH CRUNCH
WHOLE DAYS, WEEKS, **MONTHS** GO BY I CAN'T ACCOUNT FOR, OR REMEMBER.
CRUNCH
CRUNCH
THIS HOUSE, THIS WOMAN, THIS CHILD... WHAT ARE THEY?
KGNK
SET
I HAVEN'T KNOWN REAL LOVE FOR TWENTY YEARS.
KLOTG
FF FF
I NEED A CHANGE... BEFORE IT'S TOO LATE...
ngmf
FF
DRIVE AWAY... JUST LEAVE EVERYTHING BEHIND... LIKE THAT... SONG...
"JUST SLIP OUT THE BACK, JACK..."
"NO NEED TO BE COY, ROY..."
I DON'T KNOW...
MONSTERS, ALIENS... OR THAT **GREEN** GUY... WHAT'S HIS NAME? GREEN ARROW?
GREEN ARROW IS A ***SUPERHERO***, ALLIE...
FLIP
HE'S A MEMBER OF THE JUSTICE LEAGUE OF AMERICA
RIGHT...
HOW COULD I FORGET?
SET
TWIST
OKAY... WELL, I GUESS JUST MONSTERS AND ALIENS, THEN

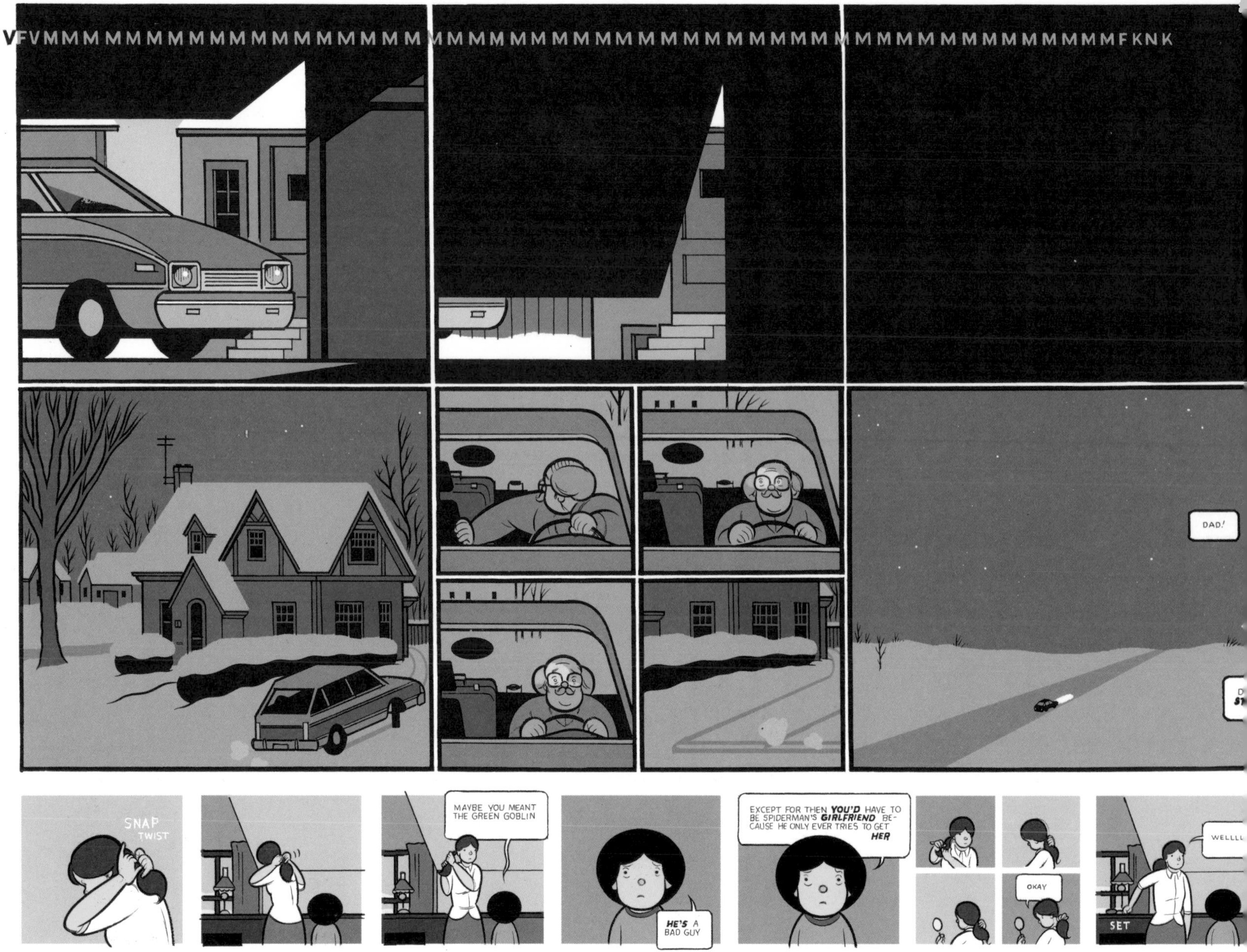
VFVMMMMMMMMMMMMMMMMMMMMMMMMMMMMMMMMMMMMMMMMMMMMMMMMMMFKNK
DAD!
SNAP
TWIST
MAYBE YOU MEANT THE GREEN GOBLIN
HE'S A BAD GUY
EXCEPT FOR THEN YOU'D HAVE TO BE SPIDERMAN'S GIRLFRIEND BE-CAUSE HE ONLY EVER TRIES TO GET HER
OKAY
SET
WELLLL

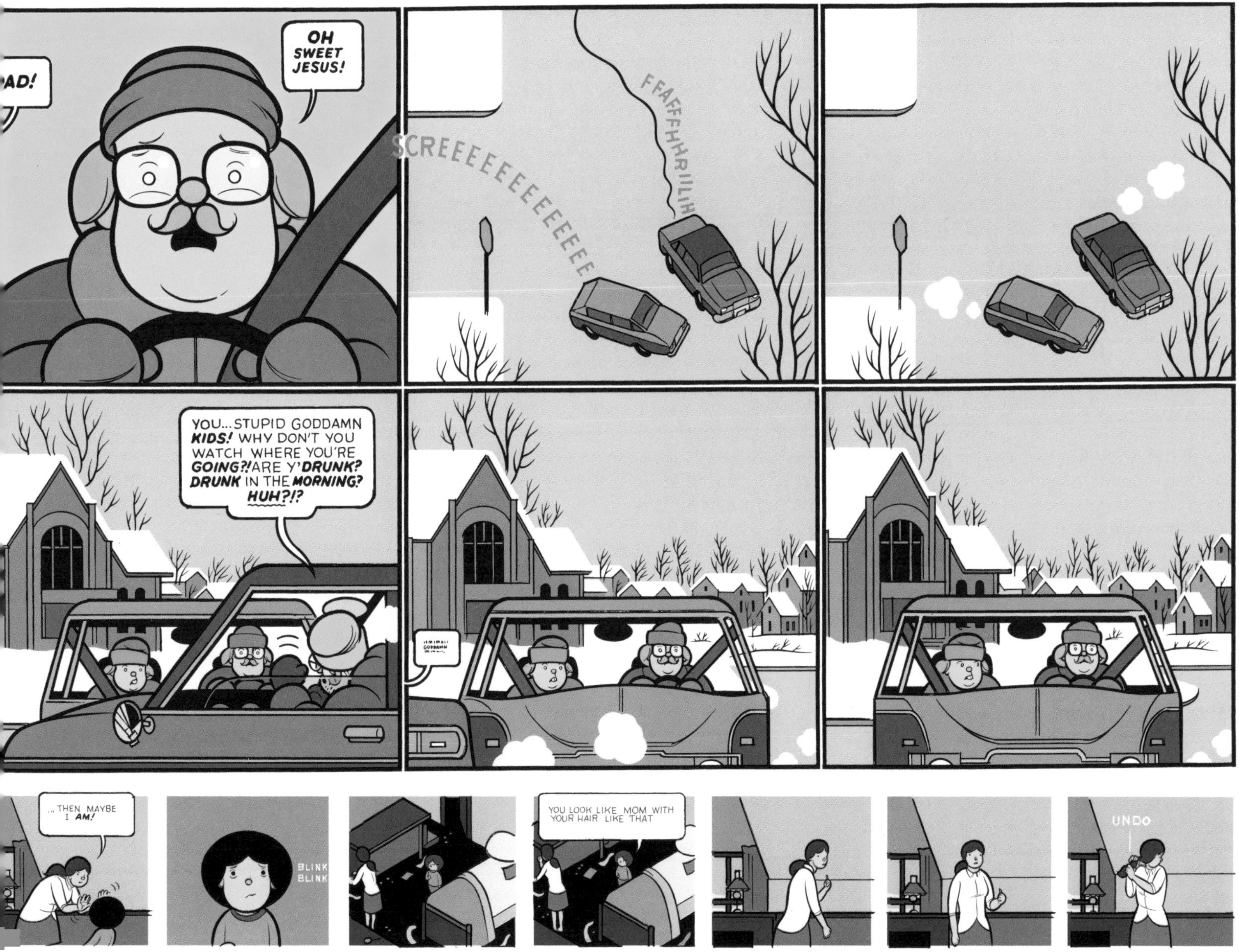
AD!
OH SWEET JESUS!
SCREEEEEEEEEEEEEEE
FFAFFFHHRIILIH
YOU...STUPID GODDAMN KIDS! WHY DON'T YOU WATCH WHERE YOU'RE GOING?! ARE Y'DRUNK? DRUNK IN THE MORNING? HUH?!?
... THEN MAYBE I AM!
BLINK BLINK
YOU LOOK LIKE MOM WITH YOUR HAIR LIKE THAT
UNDO

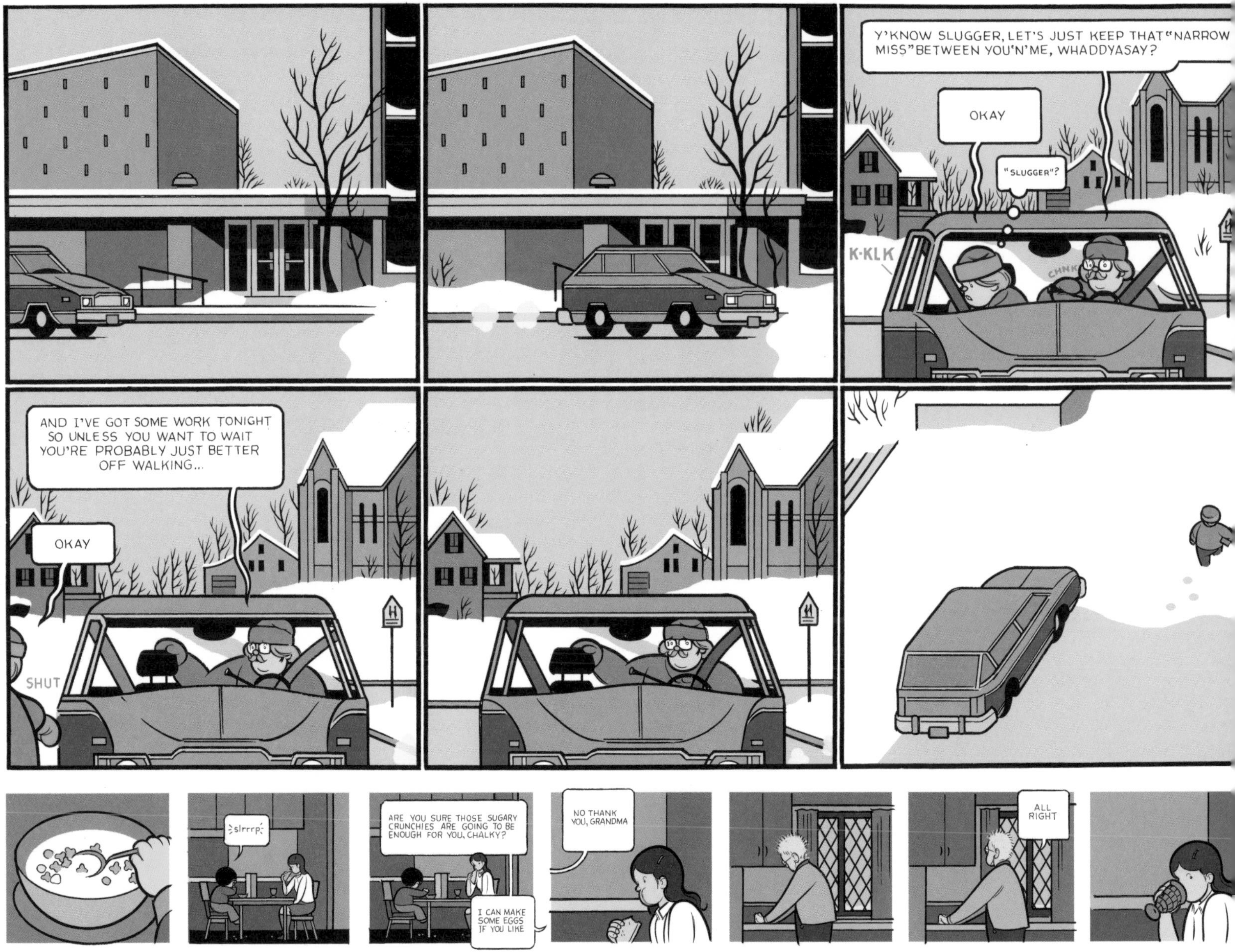

Y'KNOW SLUGGER, LET'S JUST KEEP THAT "NARROW MISS" BETWEEN YOU'N'ME, WHADDYASAY?
OKAY
"SLUGGER"?
K·KLK
CHNK
AND I'VE GOT SOME WORK TONIGHT SO UNLESS YOU WANT TO WAIT YOU'RE PROBABLY JUST BETTER OFF WALKING...
OKAY
SHUT
slrrrp
ARE YOU SURE THOSE SUGARY CRUNCHIES ARE GOING TO BE ENOUGH FOR YOU, CHALKY?
I CAN MAKE SOME EGGS IF YOU LIKE
NO THANK YOU, GRANDMA
ALL RIGHT

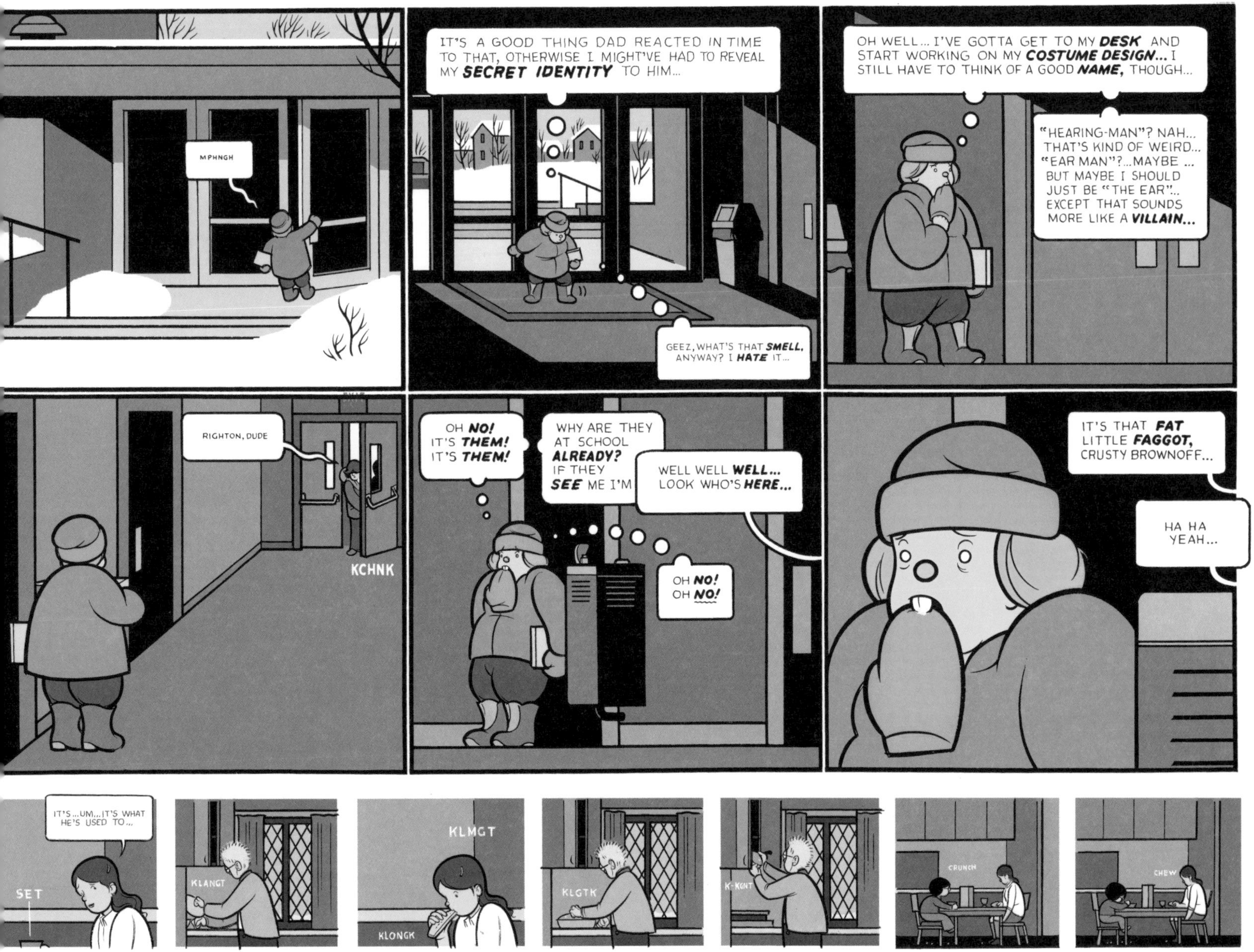

MPHNGH
IT'S A GOOD THING DAD REACTED IN TIME TO THAT, OTHERWISE I MIGHT'VE HAD TO REVEAL MY SECRET IDENTITY TO HIM...
GEEZ, WHAT'S THAT SMELL, ANYWAY? I HATE IT...
OH WELL... I'VE GOTTA GET TO MY DESK AND START WORKING ON MY COSTUME DESIGN... I STILL HAVE TO THINK OF A GOOD NAME, THOUGH...
"HEARING-MAN"? NAH... THAT'S KIND OF WEIRD... "EAR MAN"?... MAYBE ... BUT MAYBE I SHOULD JUST BE "THE EAR"... EXCEPT THAT SOUNDS MORE LIKE A VILLAIN...
RIGHTON, DUDE
KCHNK
OH NO! IT'S THEM! IT'S THEM!
WHY ARE THEY AT SCHOOL ALREADY? IF THEY SEE ME I'M
WELL WELL WELL... LOOK WHO'S HERE...
OH NO! OH NO!
IT'S THAT FAT LITTLE FAGGOT, CRUSTY BROWNOFF...
HA HA YEAH...
IT'S ...UM... IT'S WHAT HE'S USED TO...
SET
KLANGT
KLMGT
KLONGK
KLGTK
K-KGNT
CRUNCH
CHEW

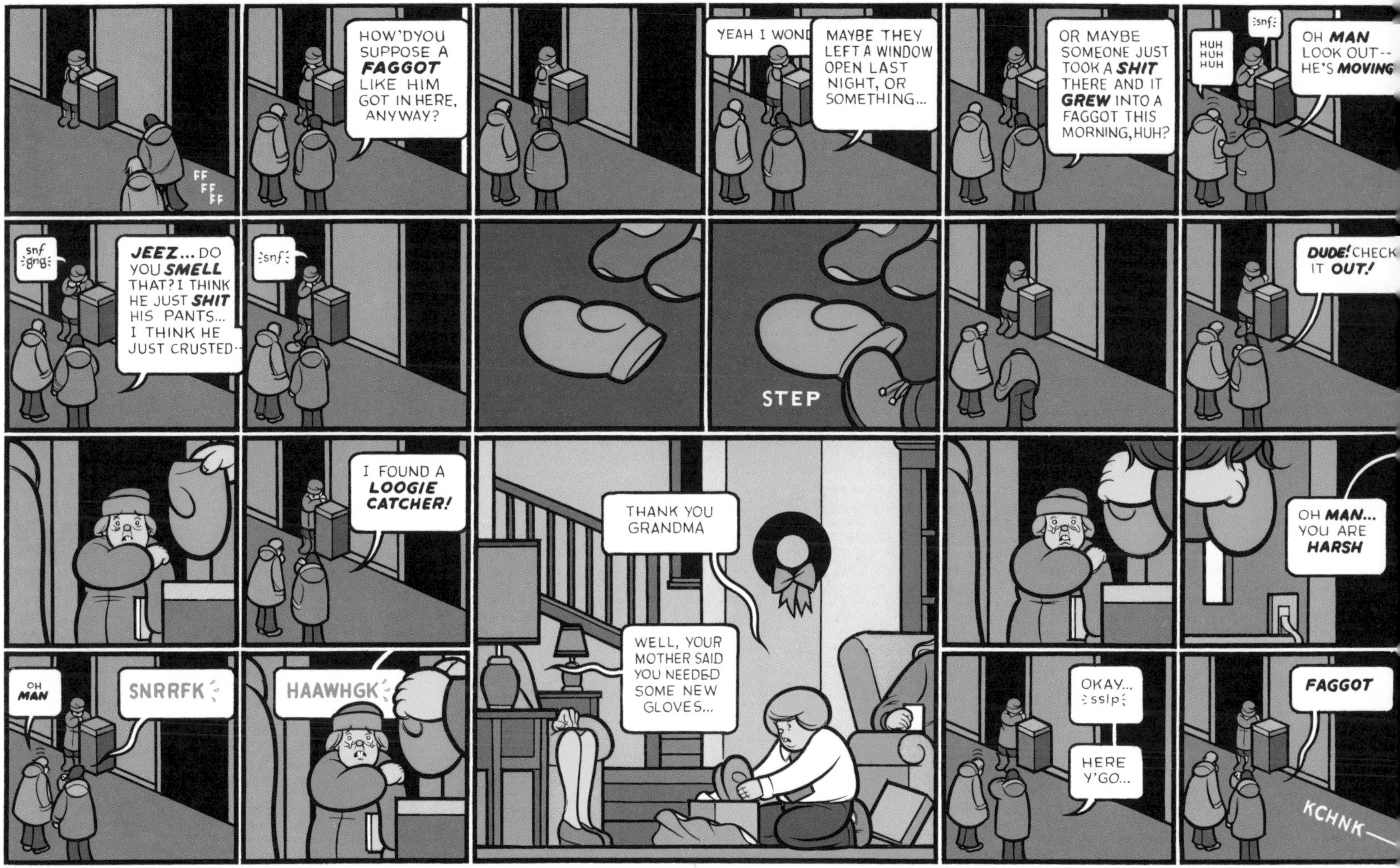
FF FF FF
HOW'DYOU SUPPOSE A FAGGOT LIKE HIM GOT IN HERE, ANYWAY?
YEAH I WOND
MAYBE THEY LEFT A WINDOW OPEN LAST NIGHT, OR SOMETHING...
OR MAYBE SOMEONE JUST TOOK A SHIT THERE AND IT GREW INTO A FAGGOT THIS MORNING, HUH?
HUH HUH HUH
snf
OH MAN LOOK OUT-- HE'S MOVING
snf gng
JEEZ... DO YOU SMELL THAT? I THINK HE JUST SHIT HIS PANTS... I THINK HE JUST CRUSTED--
snf
STEP
DUDE! CHECK IT OUT!
I FOUND A LOOGIE CATCHER!
THANK YOU GRANDMA
WELL, YOUR MOTHER SAID YOU NEEDED SOME NEW GLOVES...
OH MAN... YOU ARE HARSH
OH MAN
SNRRFK
HAAWHGK
OKAY... sslp
HERE Y'GO...
FAGGOT
KCHNK—

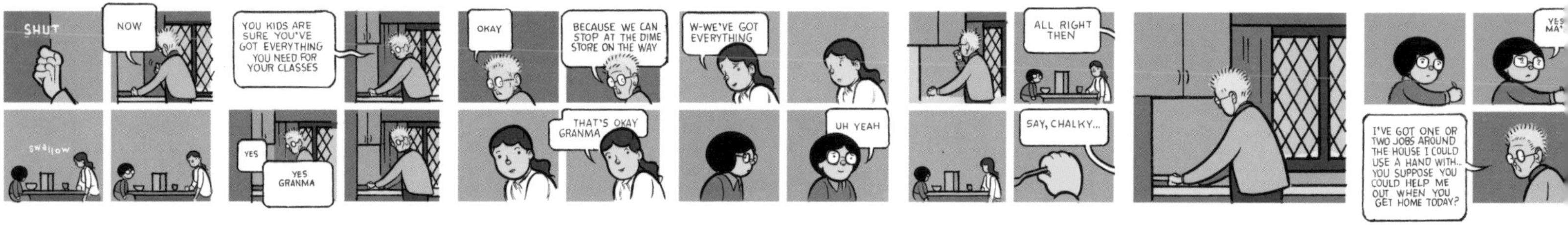
SHUT
NOW
swallow
YOU KIDS ARE SURE YOU'VE GOT EVERYTHING YOU NEED FOR YOUR CLASSES
YES
YES GRANMA
OKAY
BECAUSE WE CAN STOP AT THE DIME STORE ON THE WAY
THAT'S OKAY GRANMA
W-WE'VE GOT EVERYTHING
UH YEAH
ALL RIGHT THEN
SAY, CHALKY...
I'VE GOT ONE OR TWO JOBS AROUND THE HOUSE I COULD USE A HAND WITH... YOU SUPPOSE YOU COULD HELP ME OUT WHEN YOU GET HOME TODAY?

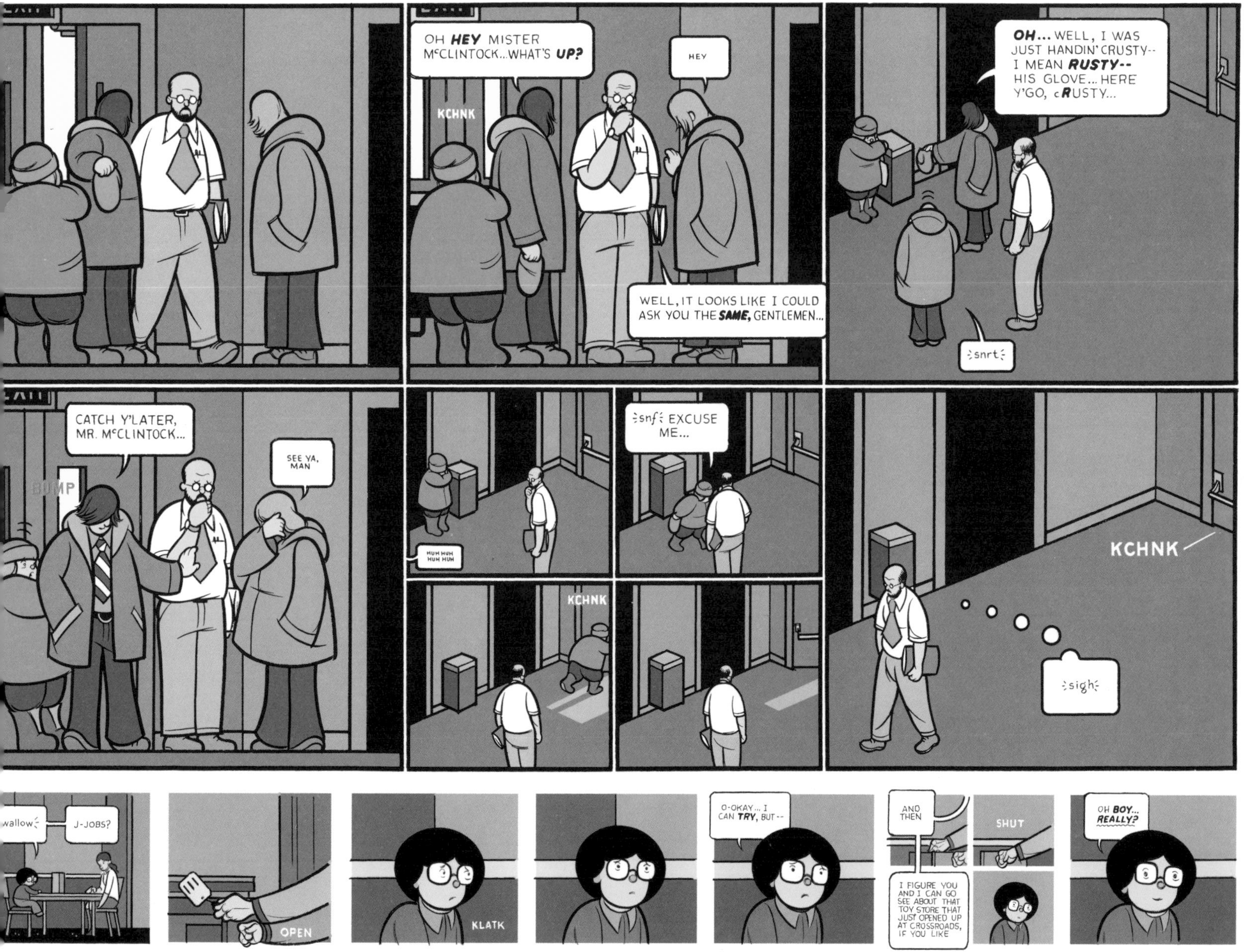
OH HEY MISTER McCLINTOCK...WHAT'S UP?
HEY
KCHNK
WELL, IT LOOKS LIKE I COULD ASK YOU THE SAME, GENTLEMEN...
OH... WELL, I WAS JUST HANDIN' CRUSTY-- I MEAN RUSTY-- HIS GLOVE... HERE Y'GO, cRUSTY...
snrt
CATCH Y'LATER, MR. McCLINTOCK...
SEE YA, MAN
BUMP
HUH HUH HUH HUH
snf EXCUSE ME...
KCHNK
KCHNK
sigh
wallow
J-JOBS?
OPEN
KLATK
O-OKAY... I CAN TRY, BUT--
AND THEN
SHUT
I FIGURE YOU AND I CAN GO SEE ABOUT THAT TOY STORE THAT JUST OPENED UP AT CROSSROADS, IF YOU LIKE
OH BOY... REALLY?

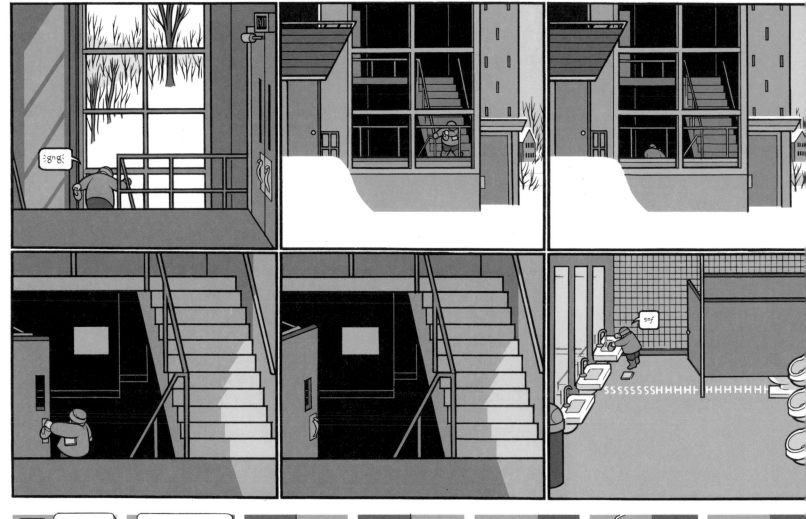

:gng:

snf

SSSSSSSSSHHHHH HHHHHHH

SURE...

BUT ONLY IF YOU PROMISE TO GIVE ME A HAND, UNDERSTAND?

I NEED A REAL **STRONGMAN'S** HELP AND I'D SAY YOU FIT **THAT** TICKET TO A "T"!

OKAY GRANDMA

AND ALISON?

YES GRANDMA

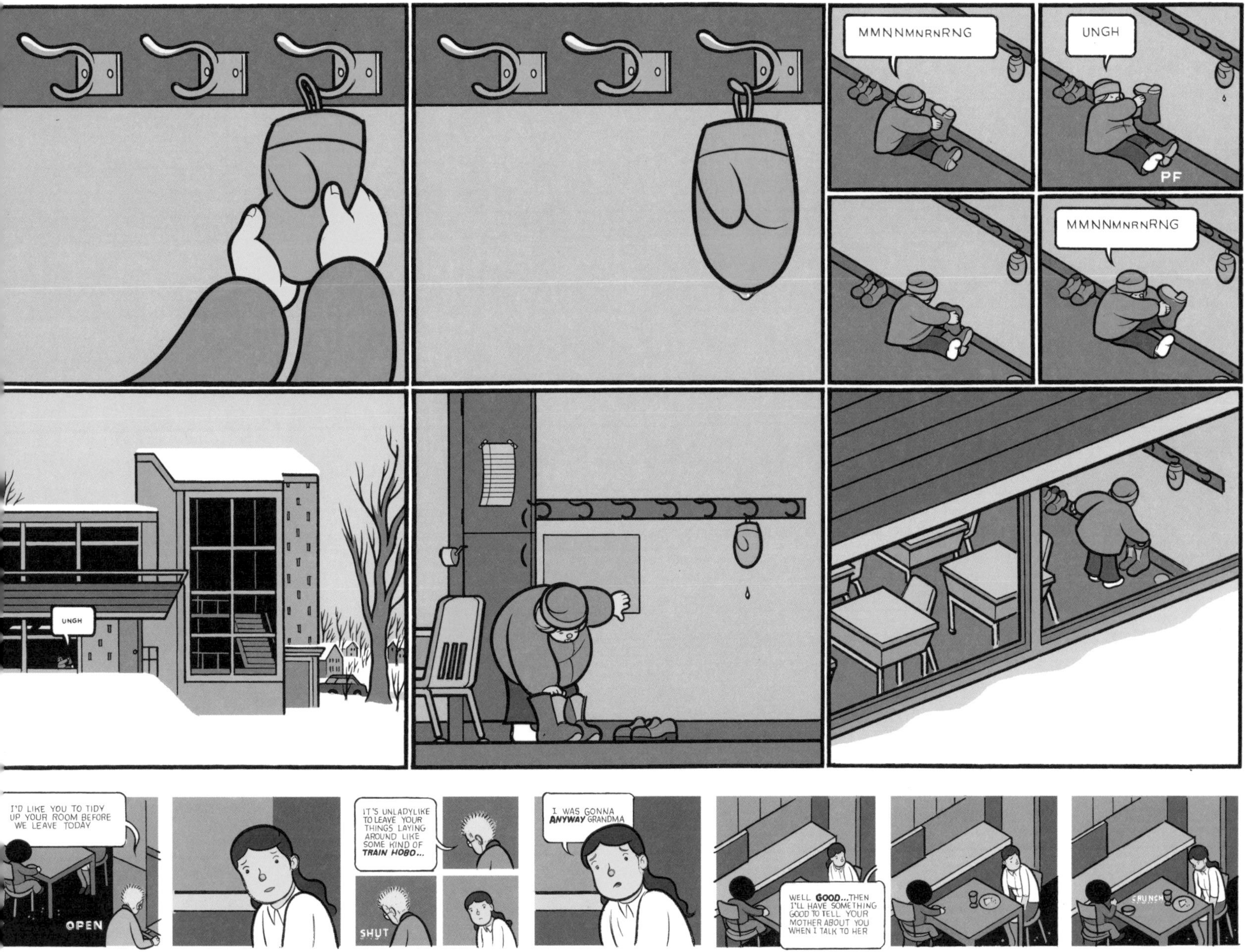
MMNNMNRNRNG
UNGH
PF
MMNNMNRNRNG
UNGH
I'D LIKE YOU TO TIDY UP YOUR ROOM BEFORE WE LEAVE TODAY
OPEN
IT'S UNLADYLIKE TO LEAVE YOUR THINGS LAYING AROUND LIKE SOME KIND OF TRAIN HOBO...
SHUT
I WAS GONNA ANYWAY GRANDMA
WELL GOOD...THEN I'LL HAVE SOMETHING GOOD TO TELL YOUR MOTHER ABOUT YOU WHEN I TALK TO HER
CRUNCH

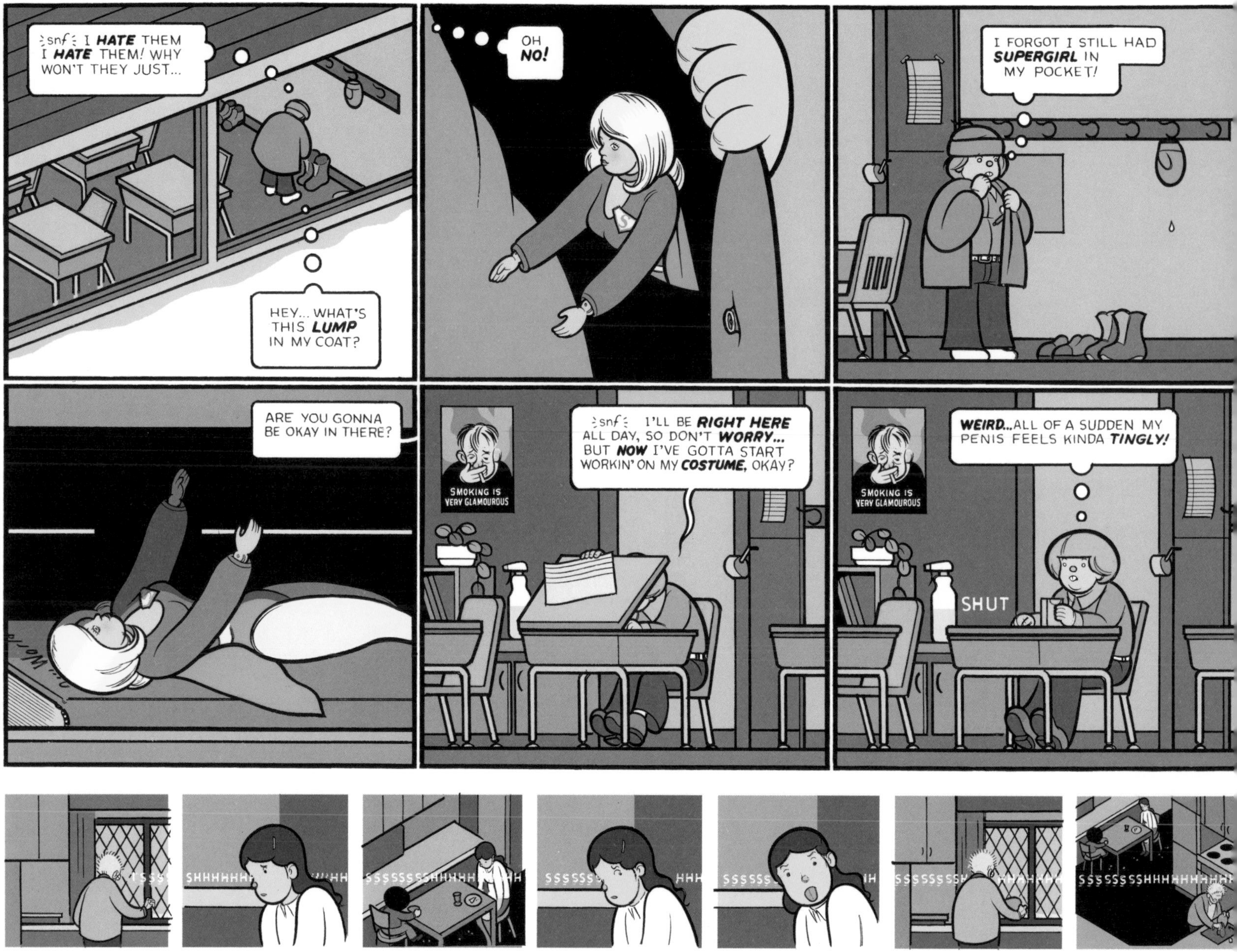

snf I HATE THEM I HATE THEM! WHY WON'T THEY JUST...
HEY... WHAT'S THIS LUMP IN MY COAT?
OH NO!
I FORGOT I STILL HAD SUPERGIRL IN MY POCKET!
ARE YOU GONNA BE OKAY IN THERE?
SMOKING IS VERY GLAMOUROUS
snf I'LL BE RIGHT HERE ALL DAY, SO DON'T WORRY... BUT NOW I'VE GOTTA START WORKIN' ON MY COSTUME, OKAY?
SMOKING IS VERY GLAMOUROUS
WEIRD...ALL OF A SUDDEN MY PENIS FEELS KINDA TINGLY!
SHUT
SHHHHHHH
SSSSSSSSHHHHHH
SSSSSS
SSSSSS
SSSSSSSSH
SSSSSSSSHHHHHHHH

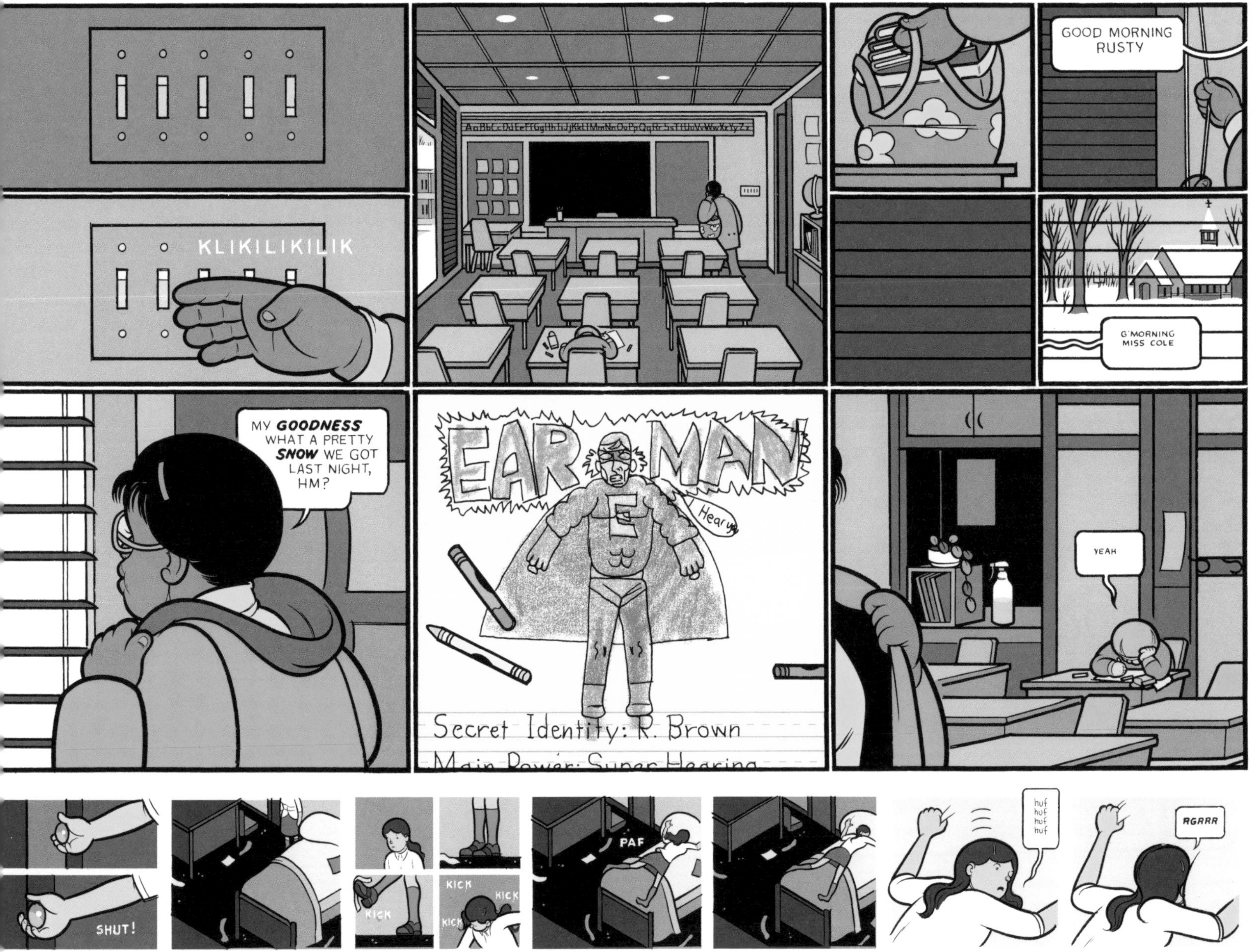
KLIKILIKILIK
GOOD MORNING RUSTY
G'MORNING MISS COLE
MY GOODNESS WHAT A PRETTY SNOW WE GOT LAST NIGHT, HM?
EAR MAN
Hear ya
Secret Identity: R. Brown
YEAH
SHUT!
KICK
KICK
KICK
KICK
PAF
huf huf huf huf
RGRRR

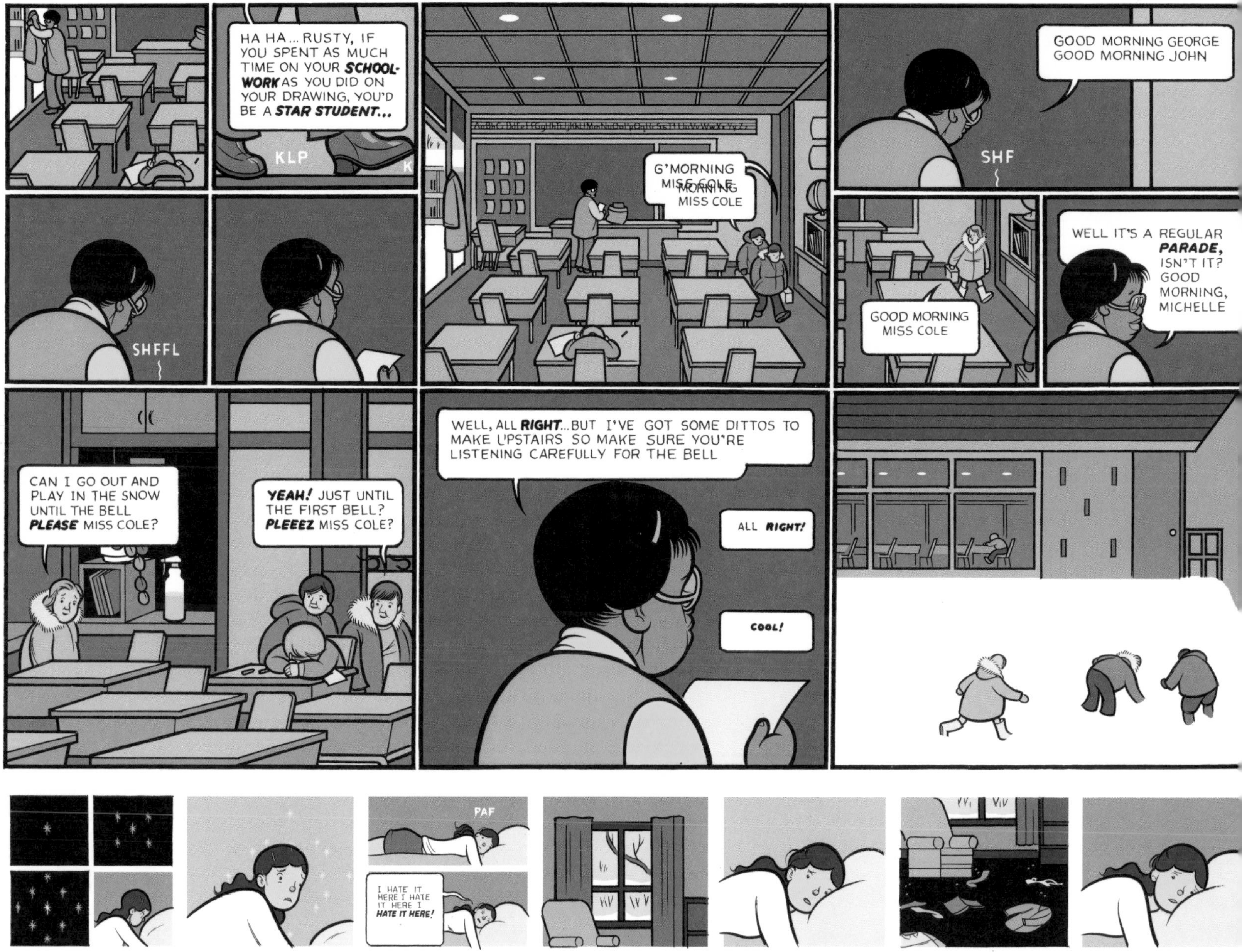
HA HA... RUSTY, IF YOU SPENT AS MUCH TIME ON YOUR **SCHOOL-WORK** AS YOU DID ON YOUR DRAWING, YOU'D BE A **STAR STUDENT...**
KLP
K
G'MORNING MISS COLE
MORNING MISS COLE
GOOD MORNING GEORGE
GOOD MORNING JOHN
SHF
SHFFL
GOOD MORNING MISS COLE
WELL IT'S A REGULAR **PARADE,** ISN'T IT? GOOD MORNING, MICHELLE
CAN I GO OUT AND PLAY IN THE SNOW UNTIL THE BELL **PLEASE** MISS COLE?
YEAH! JUST UNTIL THE FIRST BELL? **PLEEEZ** MISS COLE?
WELL, ALL **RIGHT**... BUT I'VE GOT SOME DITTOS TO MAKE UPSTAIRS SO MAKE SURE YOU'RE LISTENING CAREFULLY FOR THE BELL
ALL **RIGHT!**
COOL!
PAF
I HATE IT HERE I HATE IT HERE I **HATE IT HERE!**

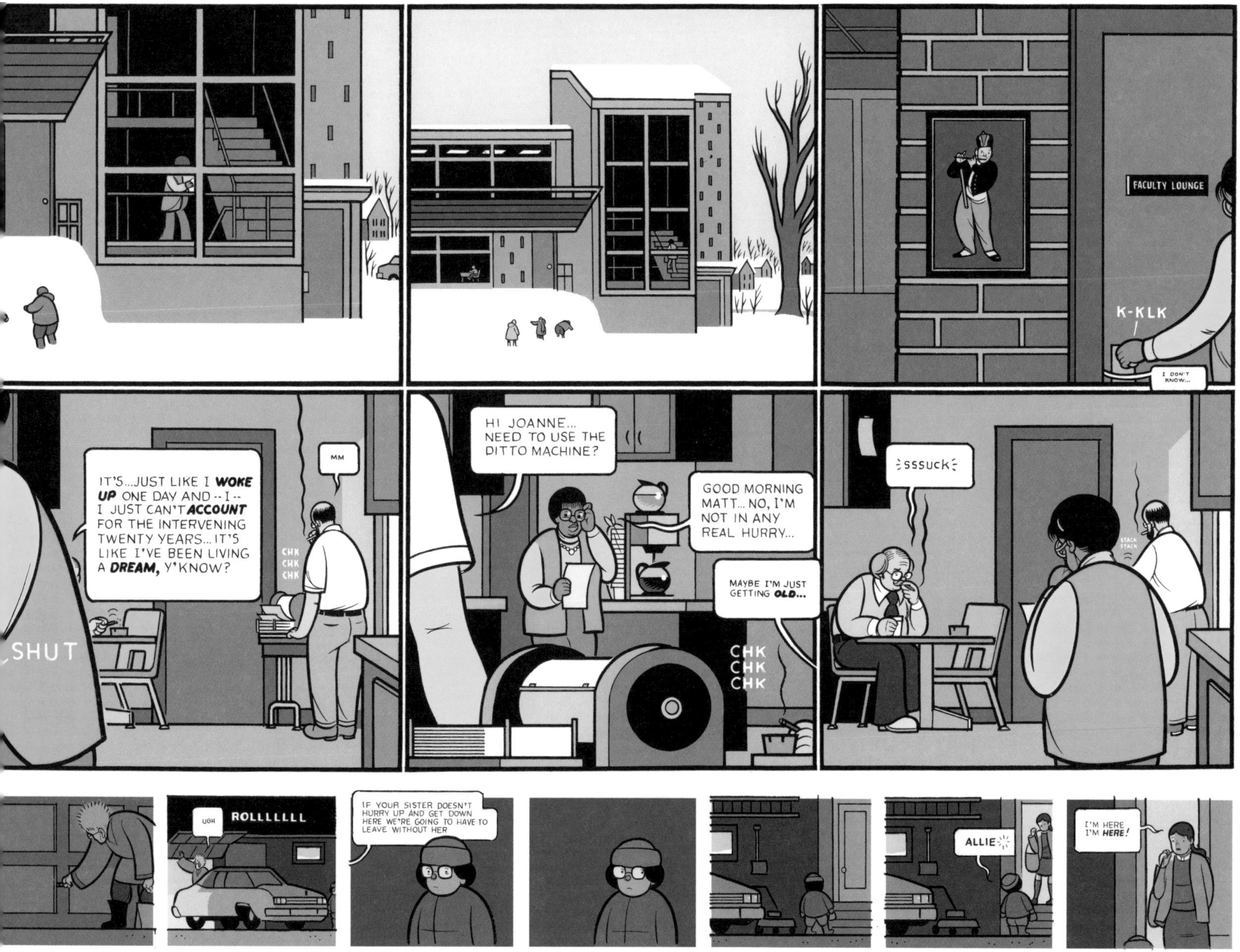
FACULTY LOUNGE
K-KLK
I DON'T KNOW...
SHUT
IT'S...JUST LIKE I WOKE UP ONE DAY AND -- I -- I JUST CAN'T ACCOUNT FOR THE INTERVENING TWENTY YEARS... IT'S LIKE I'VE BEEN LIVING A DREAM, Y'KNOW?
MM
CHK CHK CHK
HI JOANNE... NEED TO USE THE DITTO MACHINE?
GOOD MORNING MATT... NO, I'M NOT IN ANY REAL HURRY...
MAYBE I'M JUST GETTING OLD...
CHK CHK CHK
sssuck
STACK STACK
UGH
ROLLLLLLL
IF YOUR SISTER DOESN'T HURRY UP AND GET DOWN HERE WE'RE GOING TO HAVE TO LEAVE WITHOUT HER
ALLIE
I'M HERE I'M HERE!

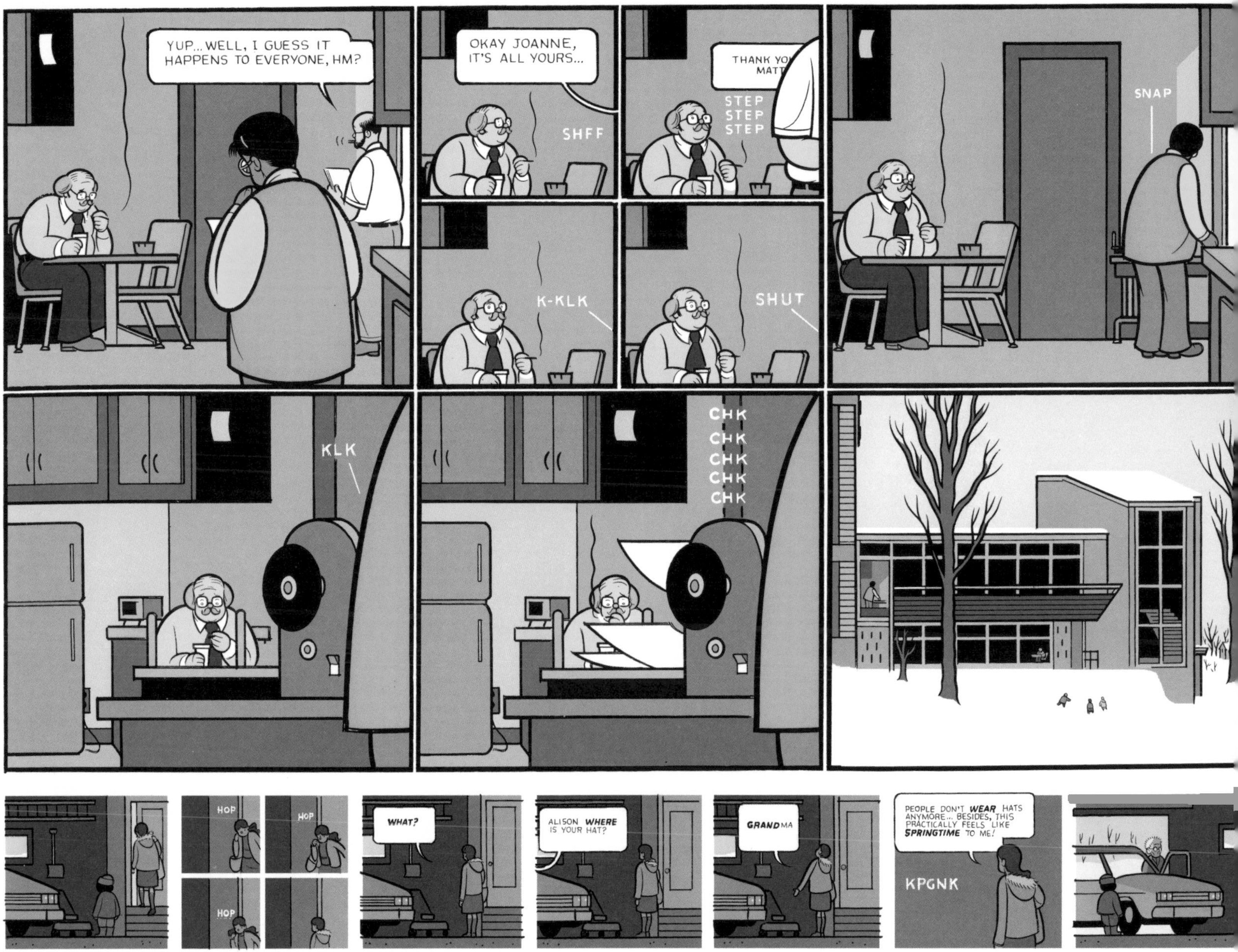
YUP... WELL, I GUESS IT HAPPENS TO EVERYONE, HM?
OKAY JOANNE, IT'S ALL YOURS...
SHFF
THANK YO
MATT
STEP
STEP
STEP
K-KLK
SHUT
SNAP
KLK
CHK
CHK
CHK
CHK
CHK
HOP
HOP
HOP
WHAT?
ALISON WHERE IS YOUR HAT?
GRANDMA
PEOPLE DON'T WEAR HATS ANYMORE... BESIDES, THIS PRACTICALLY FEELS LIKE SPRINGTIME TO ME!
KPGNK

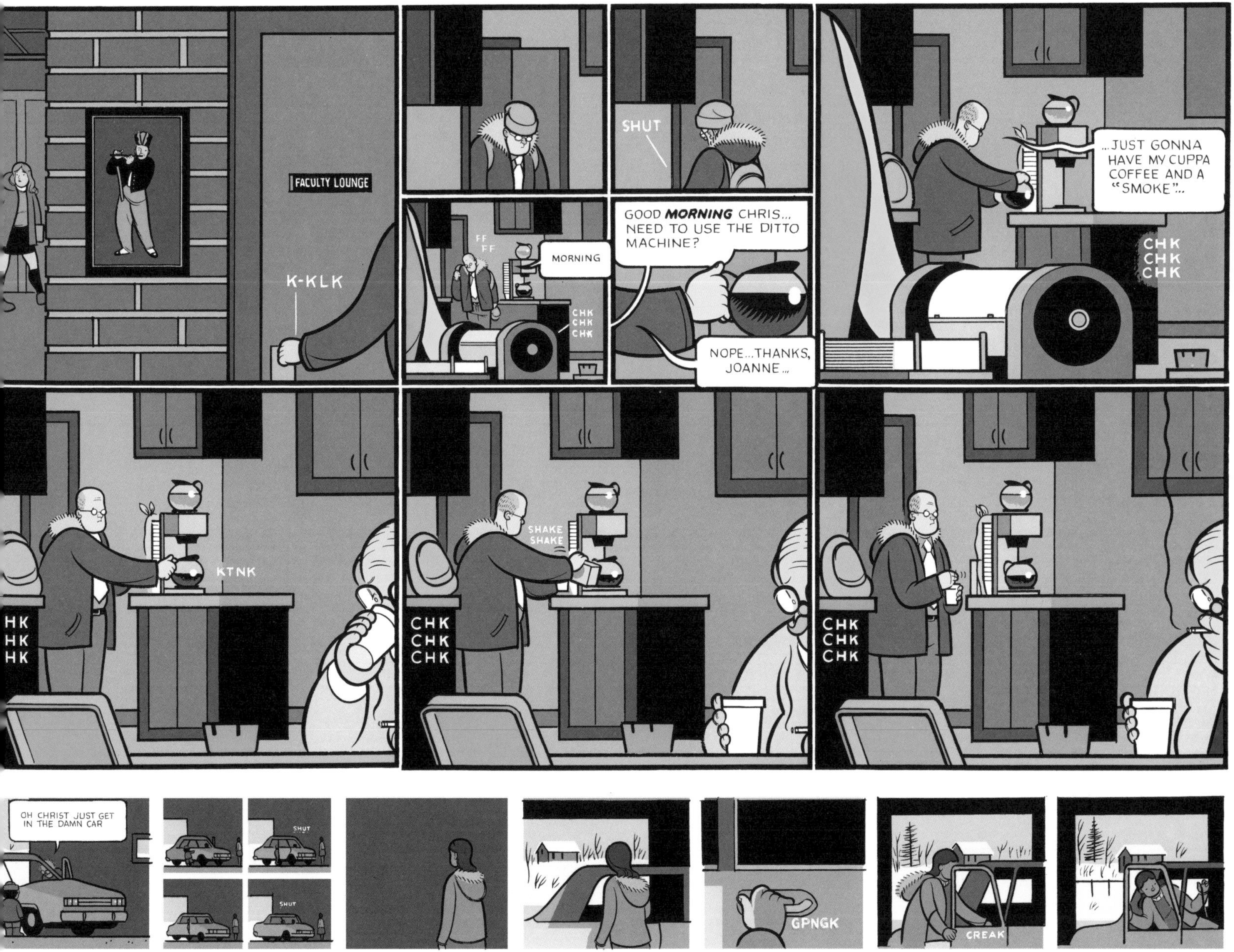
FACULTY LOUNGE
K-KLK
SHUT
FF
FF
MORNING
CHK
CHK
CHK
GOOD ***MORNING*** CHRIS... NEED TO USE THE DITTO MACHINE?
NOPE...THANKS, JOANNE...
...JUST GONNA HAVE MY CUPPA COFFEE AND A "SMOKE"...
CHK
CHK
CHK
HK
HK
HK
KTNK
SHAKE
SHAKE
CHK
CHK
CHK
CHK
CHK
CHK
OH CHRIST JUST GET IN THE DAMN CAR
SHUT
SHUT
GPNGK
CREAK

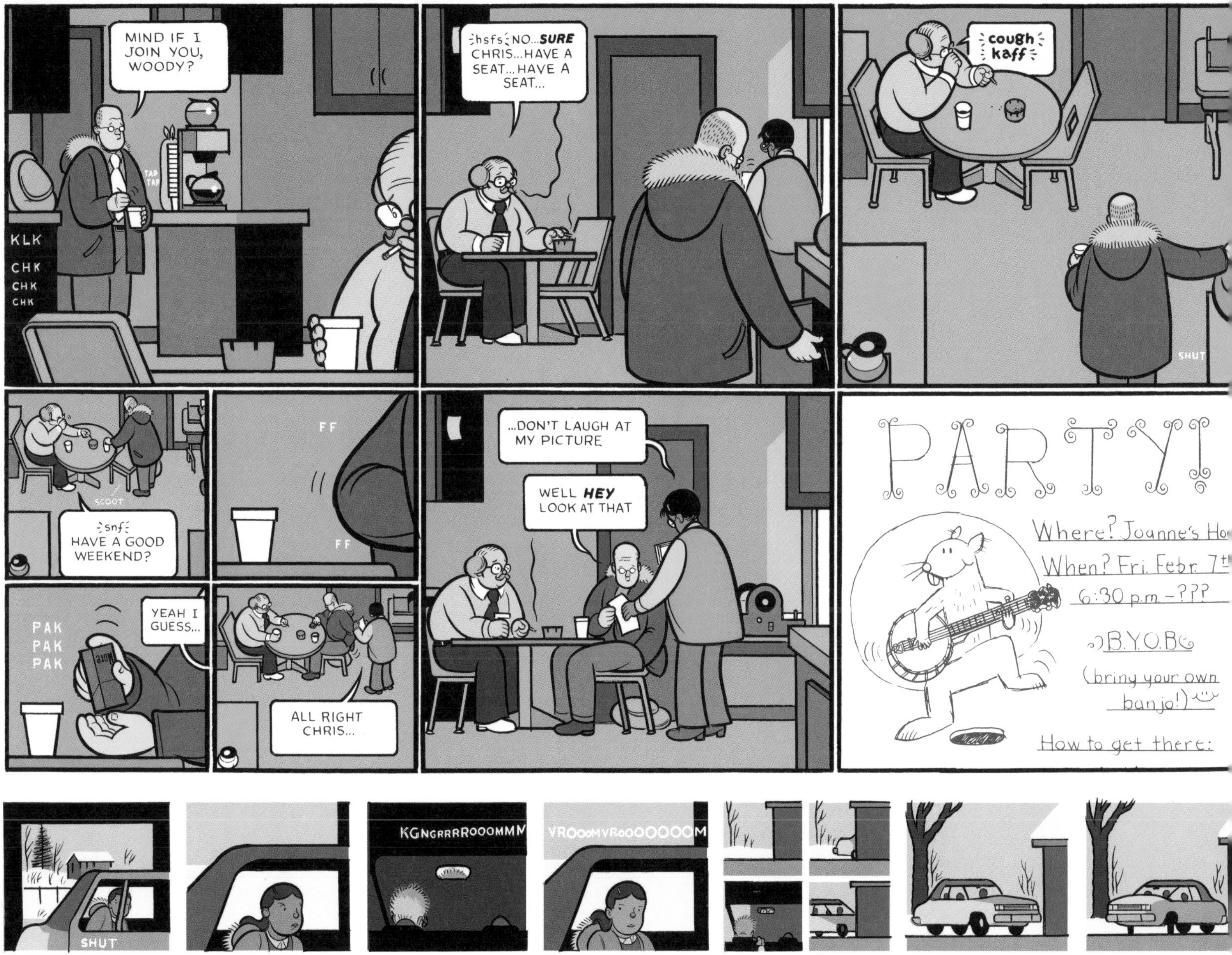

MIND IF I JOIN YOU, WOODY?
TAP TAP
KLK
CHK
CHK
CHK
hsfs NO... SURE CHRIS... HAVE A SEAT... HAVE A SEAT...
cough kaff
SHUT
SCOOT
snf HAVE A GOOD WEEKEND?
FF
FF
...DON'T LAUGH AT MY PICTURE
WELL HEY LOOK AT THAT
PARTY!
Where? Joanne's Ho
When? Fri. Febr. 7t
6:30 p.m. - ???
B.Y.O.B.
(bring your own banjo!)
How to get there:
PAK
PAK
PAK
YEAH I GUESS...
ALL RIGHT CHRIS...
SHUT
KGNGRRRROOOMMM
VROOOMVROOOOOOOOM

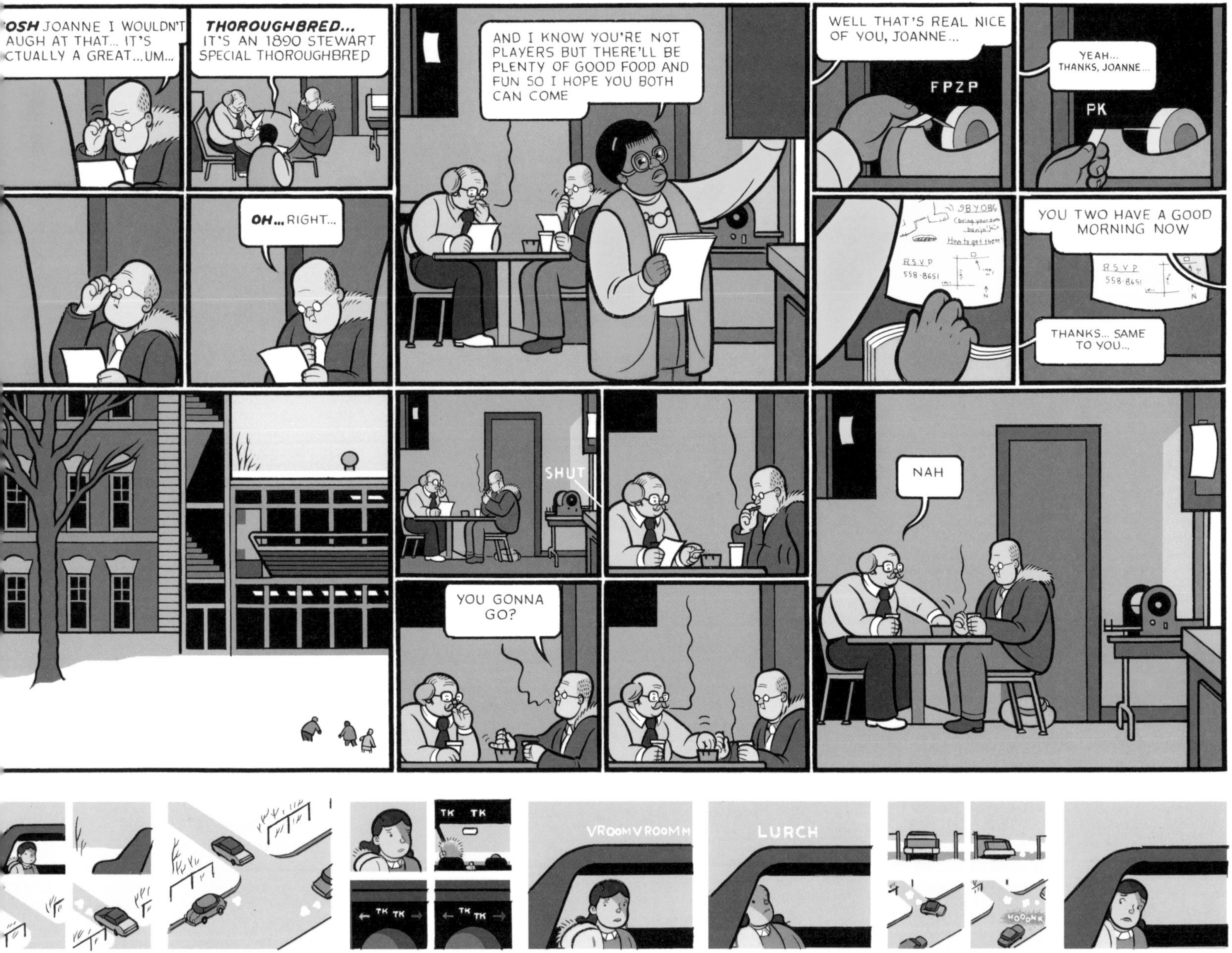
OSH JOANNE I WOULDN'T AUGH AT THAT... IT'S CTUALLY A GREAT...UM...
THOROUGHBRED... IT'S AN 1890 STEWART SPECIAL THOROUGHBRED
AND I KNOW YOU'RE NOT PLAYERS BUT THERE'LL BE PLENTY OF GOOD FOOD AND FUN SO I HOPE YOU BOTH CAN COME
WELL THAT'S REAL NICE OF YOU, JOANNE...
FPZP
YEAH... THANKS, JOANNE...
PK
OH... RIGHT...
How to get there
RSVP
558-8651
YOU TWO HAVE A GOOD MORNING NOW
RSVP
558-8651
THANKS... SAME TO YOU...
SHUT
YOU GONNA GO?
NAH
TK TK
TK TK
TK TK
VROOMVROOMM
LURCH
HOOONK

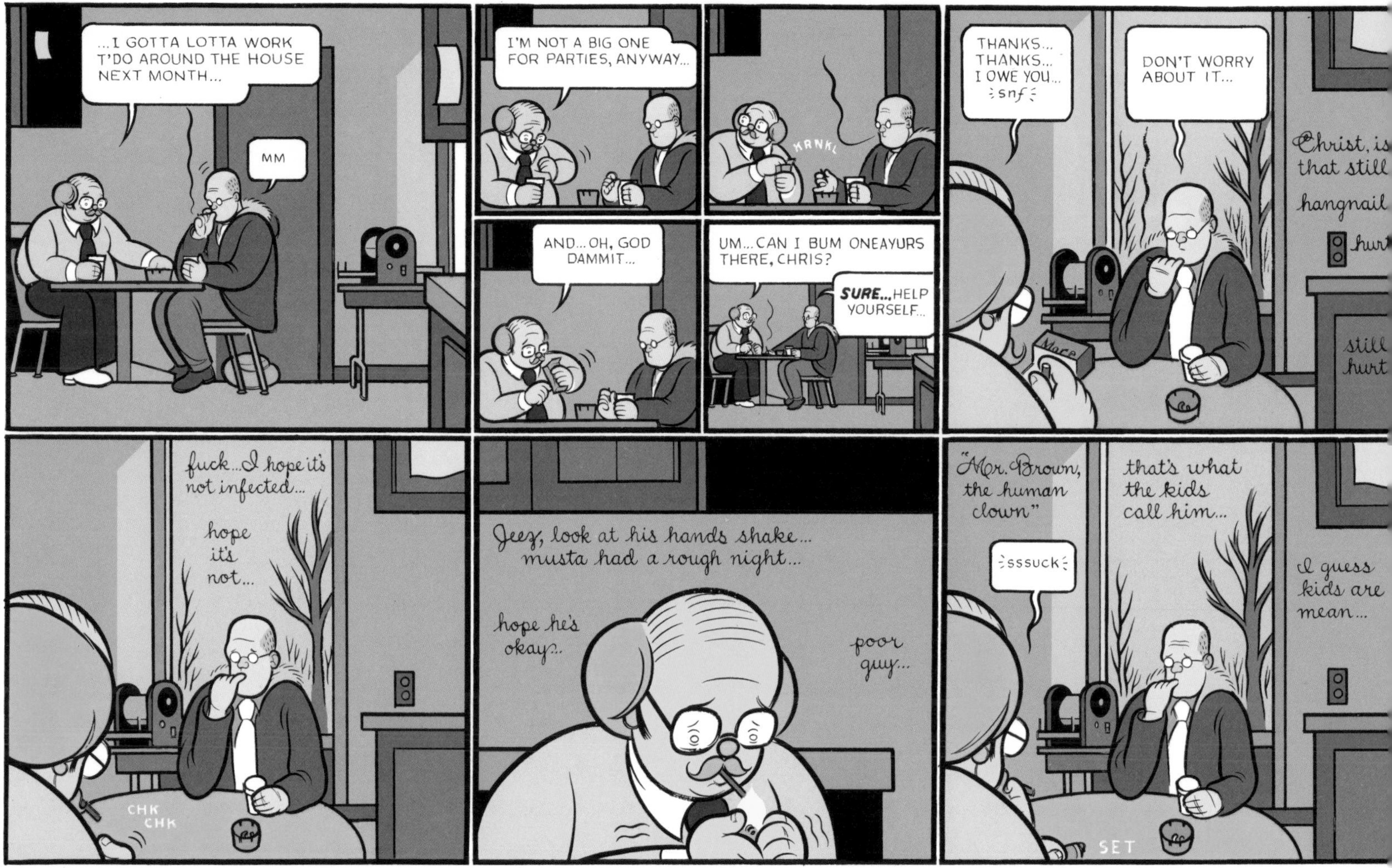
...I GOTTA LOTTA WORK T'DO AROUND THE HOUSE NEXT MONTH...
MM
I'M NOT A BIG ONE FOR PARTIES, ANYWAY...
KRNKL
AND...OH, GOD DAMMIT...
UM...CAN I BUM ONEAYURS THERE, CHRIS?
SURE...HELP YOURSELF...
THANKS... THANKS... I OWE YOU... snf
DON'T WORRY ABOUT IT...
Christ, is that still
hangnail
hurt
still hurt
fuck...I hope it's not infected...
hope it's not...
CHK CHK
Jeez, look at his hands shake... musta had a rough night...
hope he's okay...
poor guy...
"Mr. Brown, the human clown"
that's what the kids call him...
sssuck
I guess kids are mean...
SET

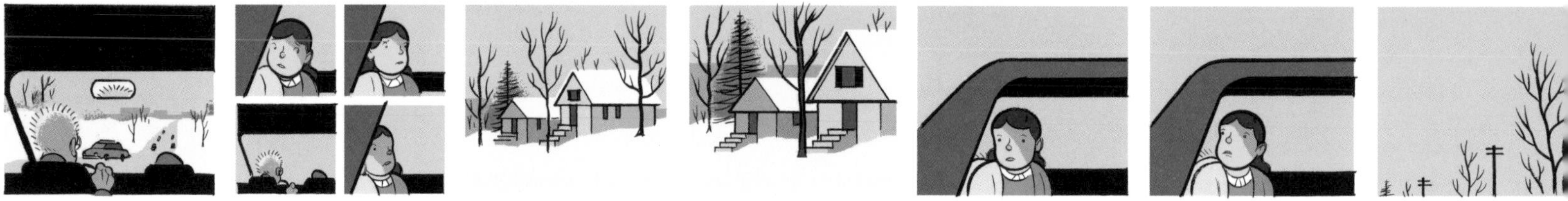

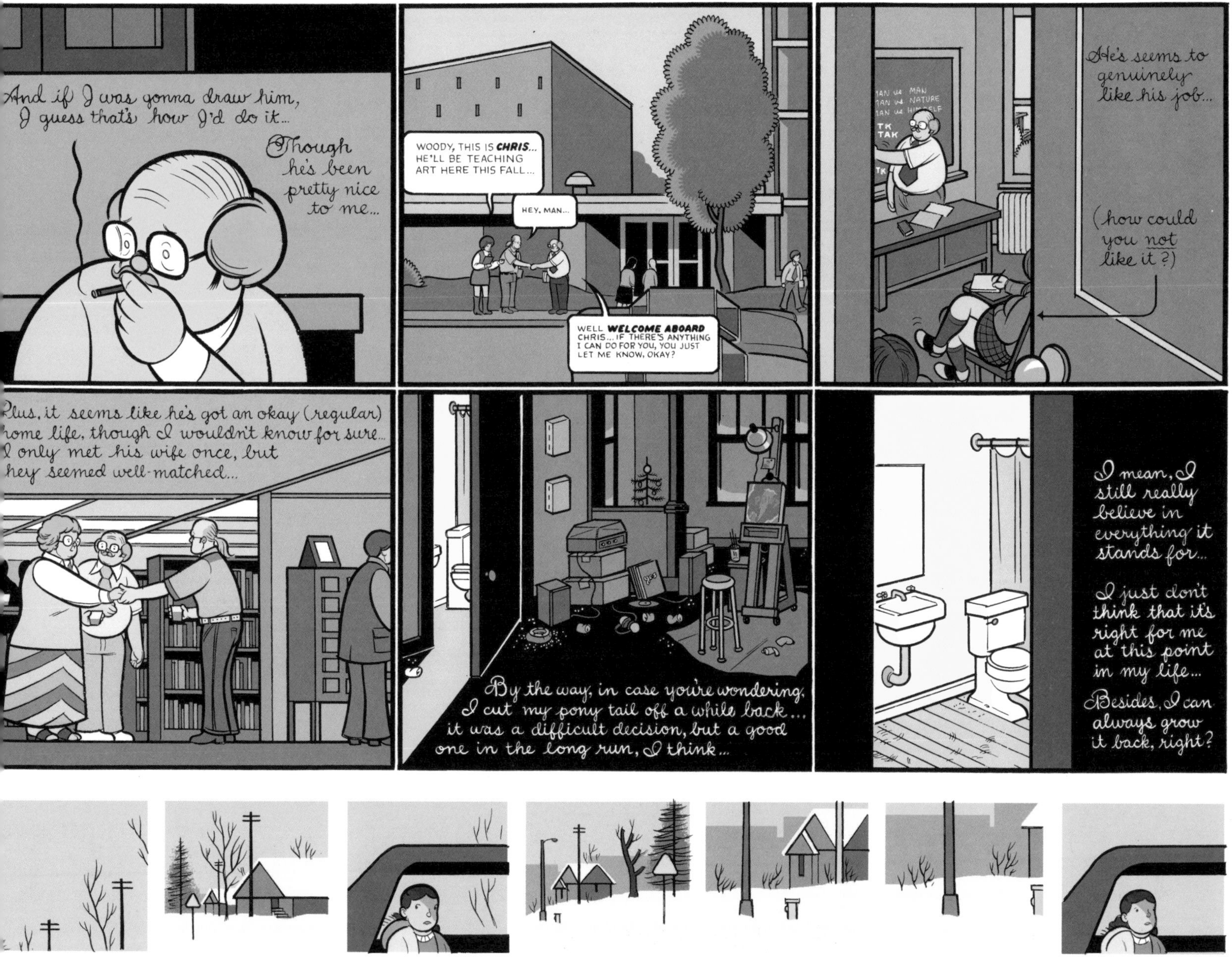
And if I was gonna draw him, I guess that's how I'd do it...
Though he's been pretty nice to me...
WOODY, THIS IS **CHRIS**... HE'LL BE TEACHING ART HERE THIS FALL...
HEY, MAN...
WELL **WELCOME ABOARD** CHRIS... IF THERE'S ANYTHING I CAN DO FOR YOU, YOU JUST LET ME KNOW, OKAY?
TK TAK
TK
He's seems to genuinely like his job...
(how could you not like it?)
Plus, it seems like he's got an okay (regular) home life, though I wouldn't know for sure... I only met his wife once, but they seemed well-matched...
By the way, in case you're wondering, I cut my pony tail off a while back... it was a difficult decision, but a good one in the long run, I think...
I mean, I still really believe in everything it stands for...
I just don't think that it's right for me at this point in my life...
Besides, I can always grow it back, right?

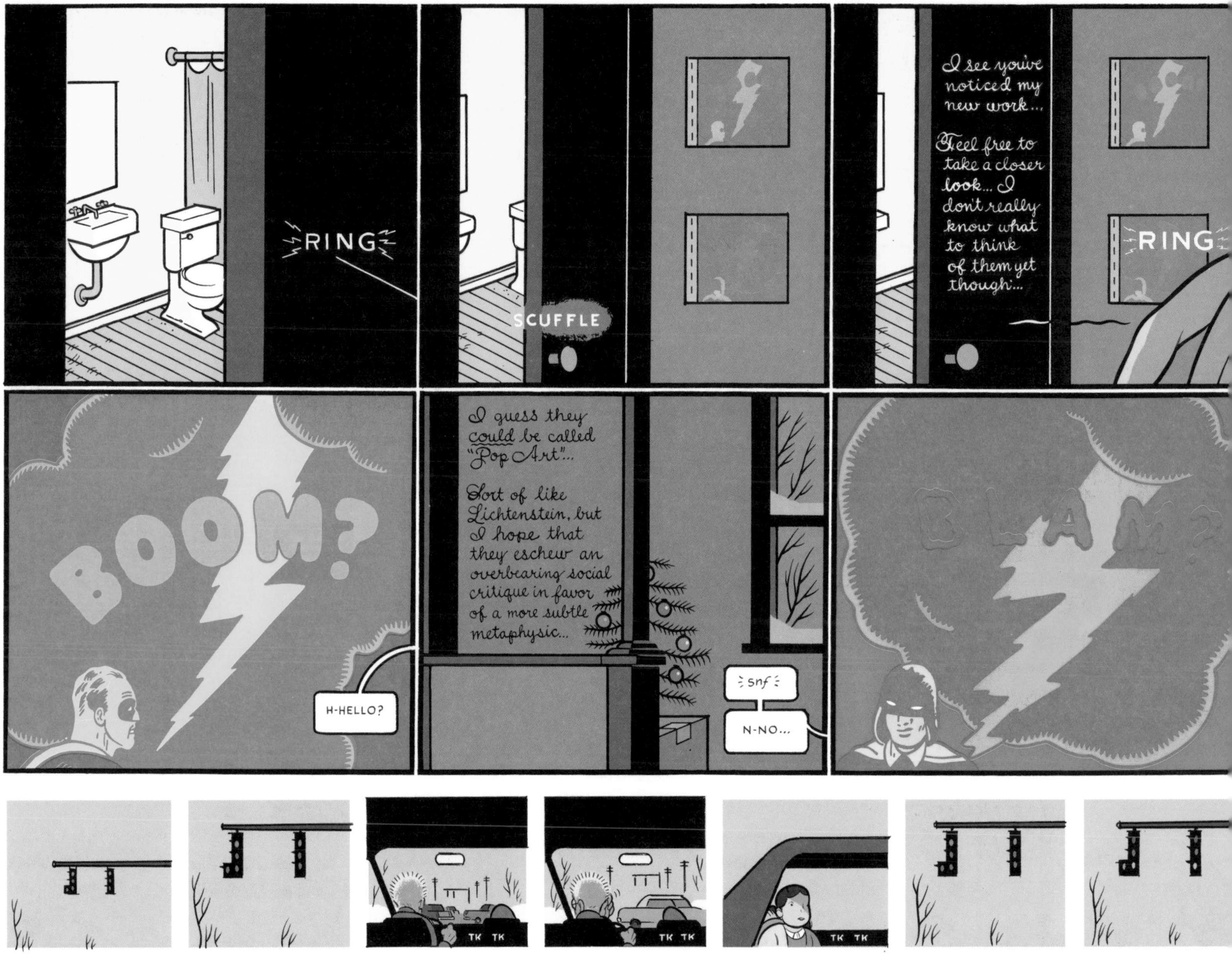

RING
SCUFFLE
I see you've noticed my new work...
Feel free to take a closer look... I don't really know what to think of them yet though...
RING
BOOM?
H-HELLO?
I guess they could be called "Pop Art"...
Sort of like Lichtenstein, but I hope that they eschew an overbearing social critique in favor of a more subtle metaphysic...
snf
N-NO...
BLAM?
TK TK
TK TK
TK TK

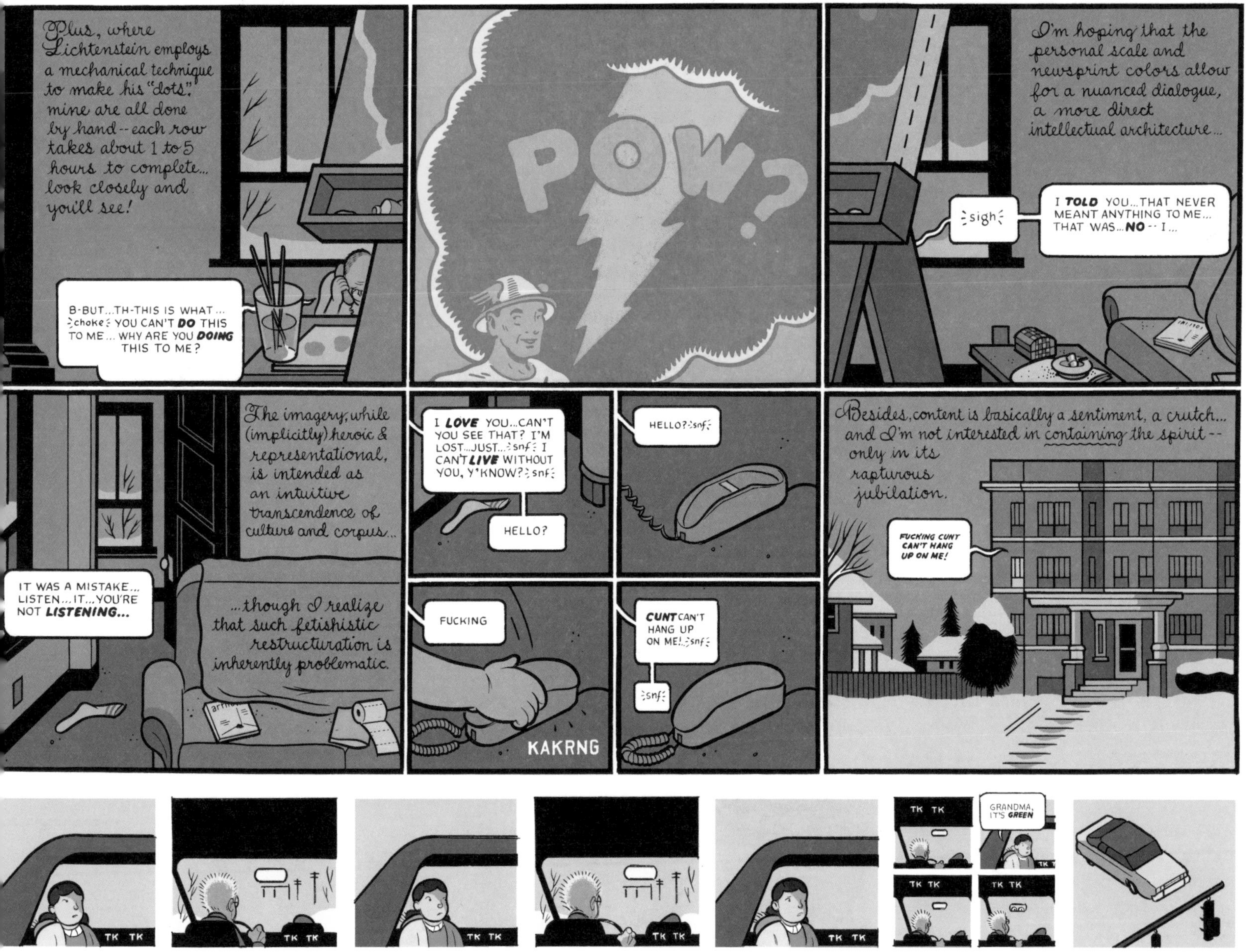

Plus, where Lichtenstein employs a mechanical technique to make his "dots," mine are all done by hand -- each row takes about 1 to 5 hours to complete... look closely and you'll see!
B-BUT... TH-THIS IS WHAT... choke YOU CAN'T DO THIS TO ME... WHY ARE YOU DOING THIS TO ME?
POW?
I'm hoping that the personal scale and newsprint colors allow for a nuanced dialogue, a more direct intellectual architecture...
sigh
I TOLD YOU... THAT NEVER MEANT ANYTHING TO ME... THAT WAS... NO -- I...
The imagery, while (implicitly) heroic & representational, is intended as an intuitive transcendence of culture and corpus...
IT WAS A MISTAKE... LISTEN... IT... YOU'RE NOT LISTENING...
...though I realize that such fetishistic restructuration is inherently problematic.
I LOVE YOU... CAN'T YOU SEE THAT? I'M LOST... JUST... snf I CAN'T LIVE WITHOUT YOU, Y'KNOW? snf
HELLO?
HELLO? snf
FUCKING
KAKRNG
CUNT CAN'T HANG UP ON ME! snf
snf
Besides, content is basically a sentiment, a crutch... and I'm not interested in containing the spirit -- only in its rapturous jubilation.
FUCKING CUNT CAN'T HANG UP ON ME!
TK TK
TK TK
TK TK
TK TK
TK TK
TK TK
GRANDMA, IT'S GREEN
TK TK
TK TK

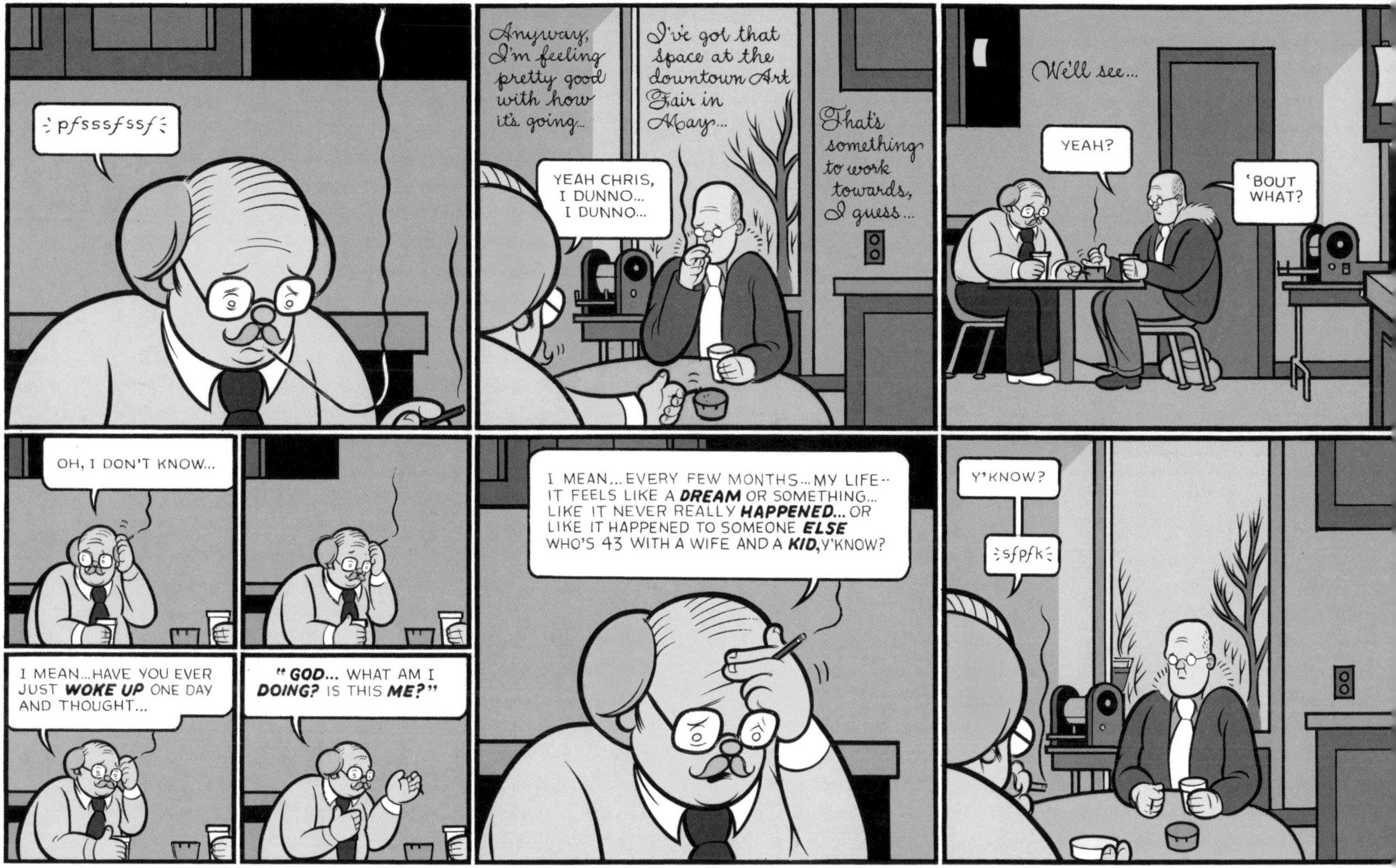
pfsssfssf
Anyway, I'm feeling pretty good with how it's going...
YEAH CHRIS, I DUNNO... I DUNNO...
I've got that space at the downtown Art Fair in May...
That's something to work towards, I guess...
We'll see...
YEAH?
'BOUT WHAT?
OH, I DON'T KNOW...
I MEAN...HAVE YOU EVER JUST **WOKE UP** ONE DAY AND THOUGHT...
"GOD... WHAT AM I **DOING?** IS THIS **ME?"**
I MEAN... EVERY FEW MONTHS... MY LIFE-- IT FEELS LIKE A **DREAM** OR SOMETHING... LIKE IT NEVER REALLY **HAPPENED...** OR LIKE IT HAPPENED TO SOMEONE **ELSE** WHO'S 43 WITH A WIFE AND A **KID,** Y'KNOW?
Y'KNOW?
sfpfk

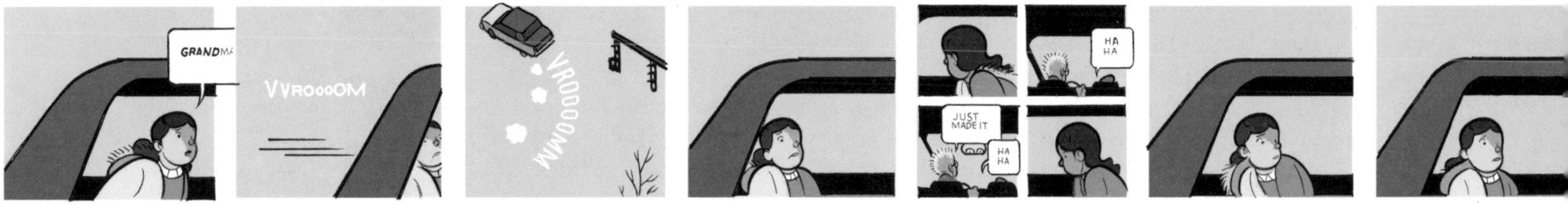
GRANDM
VVROooOM
VROOOOMM
HA HA
JUST MADE IT
HA HA

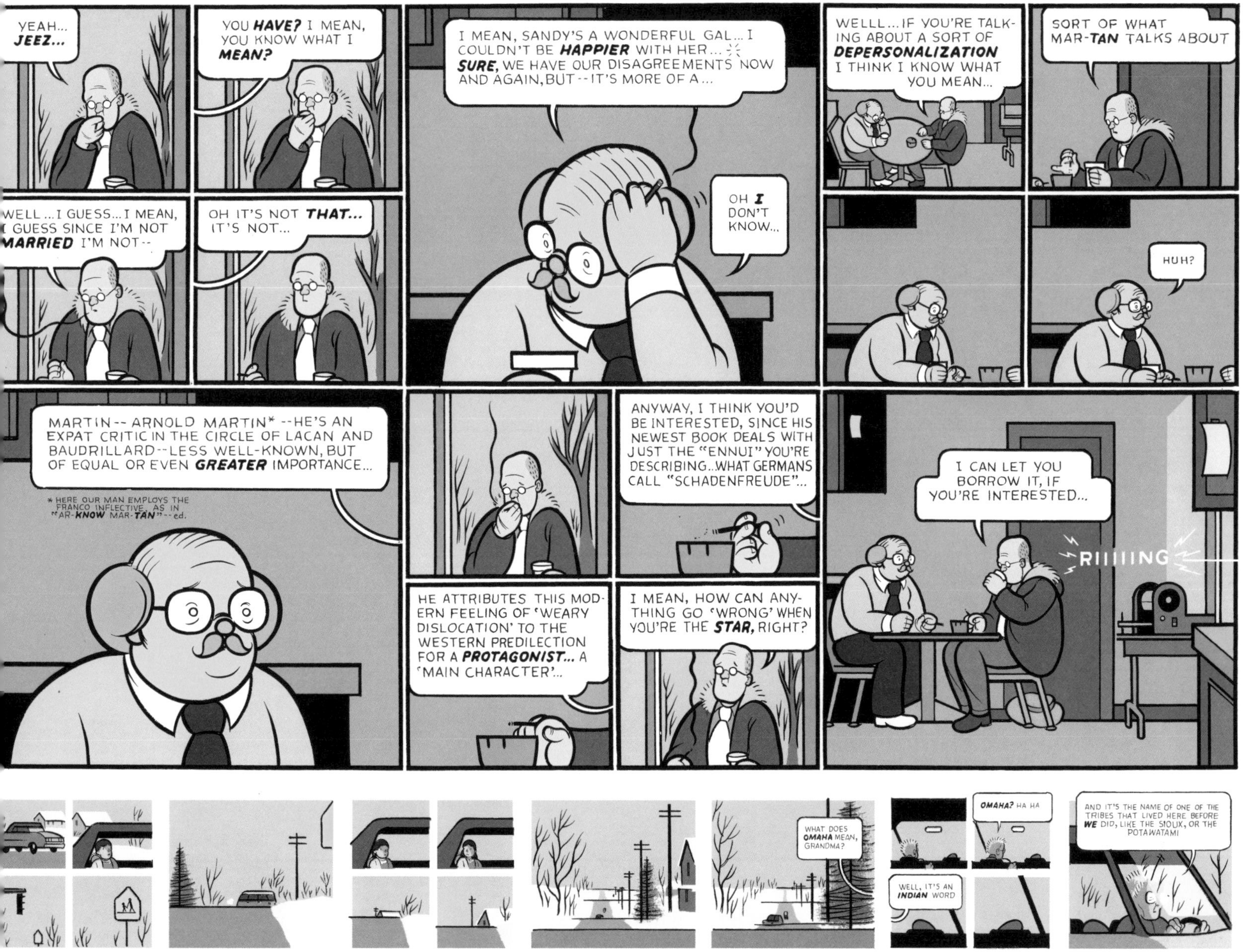
YEAH... **JEEZ...**
YOU **HAVE?** I MEAN, YOU KNOW WHAT I **MEAN?**
WELL... I GUESS... I MEAN, I GUESS SINCE I'M NOT **MARRIED** I'M NOT--
OH IT'S NOT **THAT...** IT'S NOT...
I MEAN, SANDY'S A WONDERFUL GAL... I COULDN'T BE **HAPPIER** WITH HER... **SURE,** WE HAVE OUR DISAGREEMENTS NOW AND AGAIN, BUT -- IT'S MORE OF A...
OH **I** DON'T KNOW...
WELLL... IF YOU'RE TALKING ABOUT A SORT OF **DEPERSONALIZATION** I THINK I KNOW WHAT YOU MEAN...
SORT OF WHAT MAR-**TAN** TALKS ABOUT
HUH?
MARTIN -- ARNOLD MARTIN* -- HE'S AN EXPAT CRITIC IN THE CIRCLE OF LACAN AND BAUDRILLARD -- LESS WELL-KNOWN, BUT OF EQUAL OR EVEN **GREATER** IMPORTANCE...
* HERE OUR MAN EMPLOYS THE FRANCO INFLECTIVE, AS IN "AR-**KNOW** MAR-**TAN**" -- ed.
ANYWAY, I THINK YOU'D BE INTERESTED, SINCE HIS NEWEST BOOK DEALS WITH JUST THE "ENNUI" YOU'RE DESCRIBING... WHAT GERMANS CALL "SCHADENFREUDE"...
HE ATTRIBUTES THIS MODERN FEELING OF 'WEARY DISLOCATION' TO THE WESTERN PREDILECTION FOR A **PROTAGONIST...** A 'MAIN CHARACTER'...
I MEAN, HOW CAN ANYTHING GO 'WRONG' WHEN YOU'RE THE **STAR,** RIGHT?
I CAN LET YOU BORROW IT, IF YOU'RE INTERESTED...
RIIIIING
WHAT DOES **OMAHA** MEAN, GRANDMA?
WELL, IT'S AN **INDIAN** WORD
OMAHA? HA HA
AND IT'S THE NAME OF ONE OF THE TRIBES THAT LIVED HERE BEFORE **WE** DID, LIKE THE SIOUX, OR THE POTAWATAMI

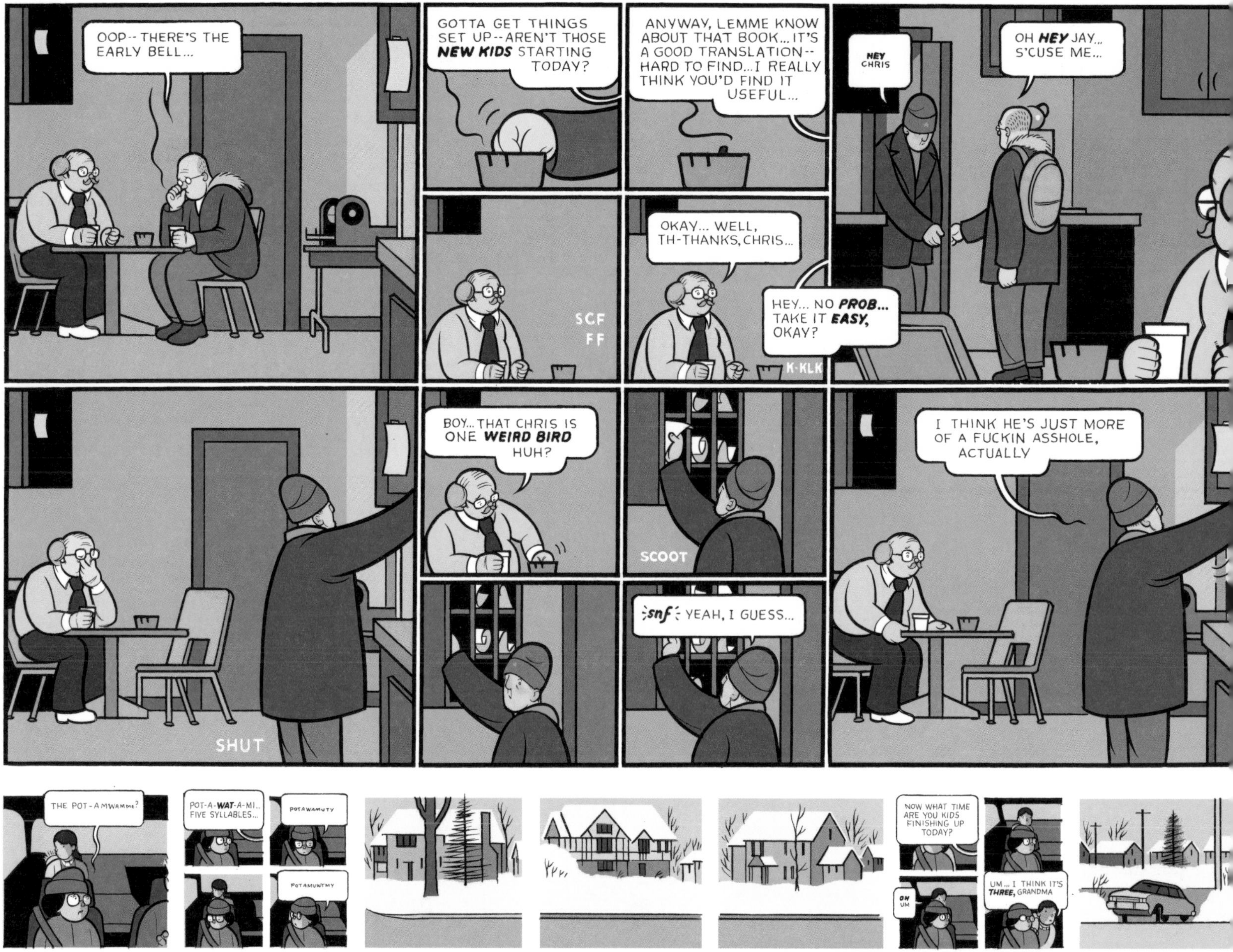
OOP-- THERE'S THE EARLY BELL...
GOTTA GET THINGS SET UP-- AREN'T THOSE **NEW KIDS** STARTING TODAY?
ANYWAY, LEMME KNOW ABOUT THAT BOOK... IT'S A GOOD TRANSLATION-- HARD TO FIND... I REALLY THINK YOU'D FIND IT USEFUL...
SCF FF
OKAY... WELL, TH-THANKS, CHRIS...
HEY... NO **PROB...** TAKE IT **EASY,** OKAY?
K-KLK
HEY CHRIS
OH **HEY** JAY... S'CUSE ME...
SHUT
BOY... THAT CHRIS IS ONE **WEIRD BIRD** HUH?
SCOOT
snf YEAH, I GUESS...
I THINK HE'S JUST MORE OF A FUCKIN ASSHOLE, ACTUALLY
THE POT-AMWAMME?
POT-A-**WAT**-A-MI... FIVE SYLLABLES...
POTAWAMUTY
POTAMUWTMY
NOW WHAT TIME ARE YOU KIDS FINISHING UP TODAY?
OH UM
UM... I THINK IT'S **THREE,** GRANDMA

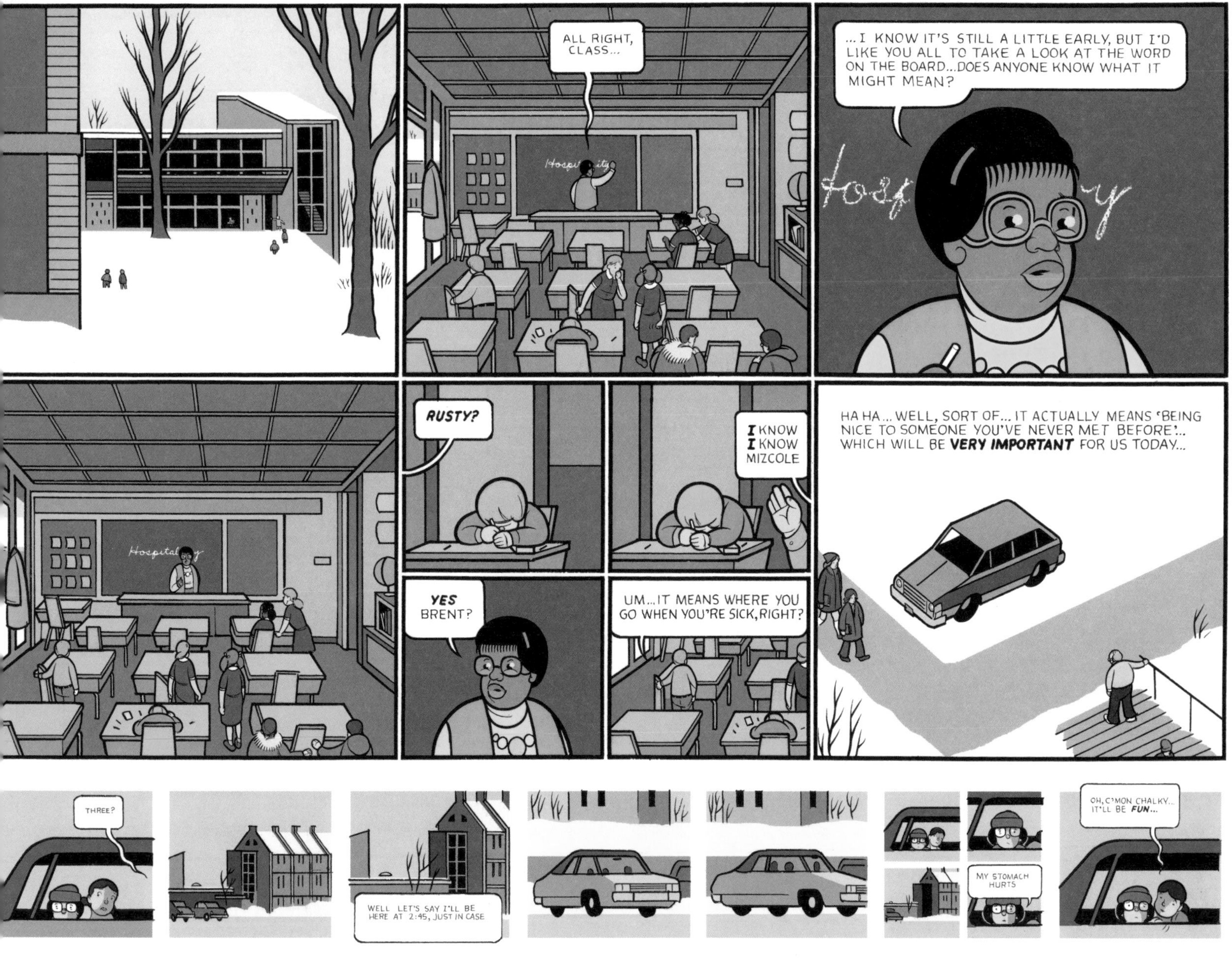
ALL RIGHT, CLASS...
...I KNOW IT'S STILL A LITTLE EARLY, BUT I'D LIKE YOU ALL TO TAKE A LOOK AT THE WORD ON THE BOARD...DOES ANYONE KNOW WHAT IT MIGHT MEAN?
RUSTY?
I KNOW I KNOW MIZCOLE
YES BRENT?
UM...IT MEANS WHERE YOU GO WHEN YOU'RE SICK, RIGHT?
HA HA... WELL, SORT OF... IT ACTUALLY MEANS 'BEING NICE TO SOMEONE YOU'VE NEVER MET BEFORE'... WHICH WILL BE VERY IMPORTANT FOR US TODAY...
THREE?
WELL LET'S SAY I'LL BE HERE AT 2:45, JUST IN CASE
MY STOMACH HURTS
OH, C'MON CHALKY... IT'LL BE FUN...

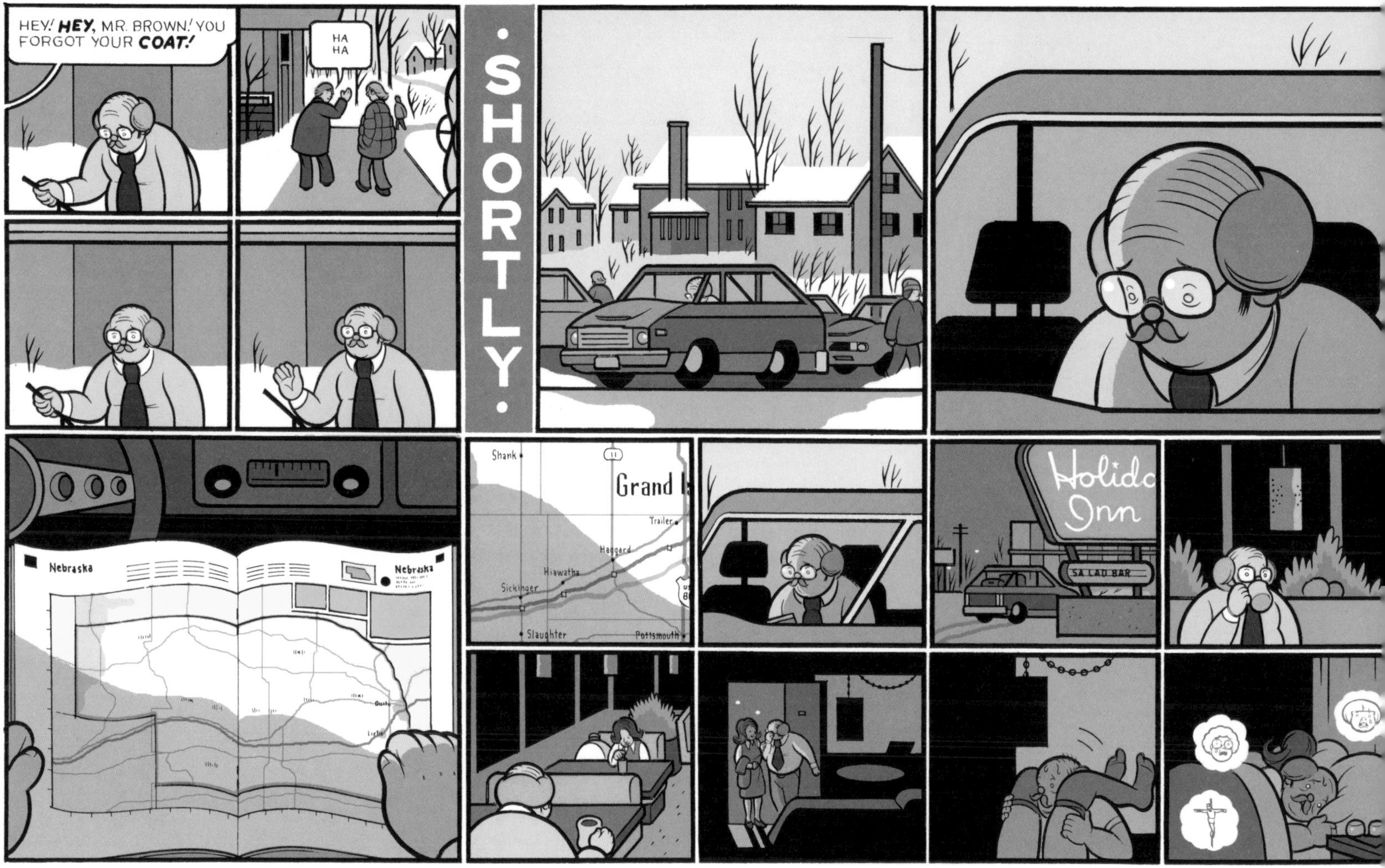
HEY! **HEY**, MR. BROWN! YOU FORGOT YOUR **COAT!**
HA HA
SHORTLY.
Shank
Grand
Trailer
Haggard
Hiawatha
Sickinger
Slaughter
Pottsmouth
Nebraska
Nebraska
Inn
SALAD BAR

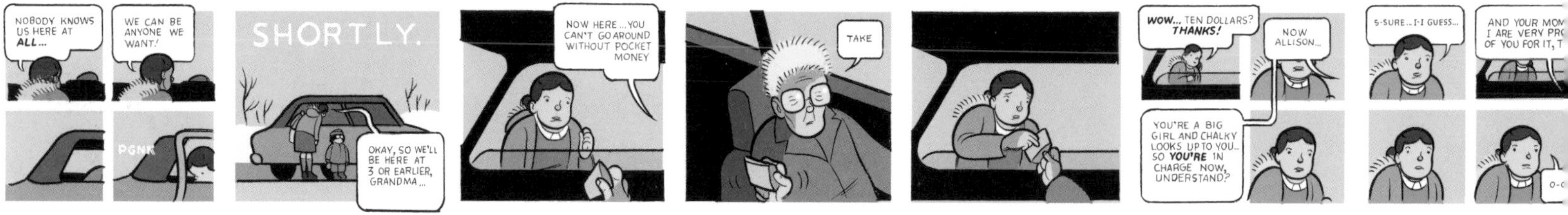
NOBODY KNOWS US HERE AT **ALL...**
WE CAN BE ANYONE WE WANT!
PGNK
SHORTLY.
OKAY, SO WE'LL BE HERE AT 3 OR EARLIER, GRANDMA...
NOW HERE... YOU CAN'T GO AROUND WITHOUT POCKET MONEY
TAKE
WOW... TEN DOLLARS? ***THANKS!***
NOW ALLISON...
YOU'RE A BIG GIRL AND CHALKY LOOKS UP TO YOU... SO **YOU'RE** IN CHARGE NOW, UNDERSTAND?
S-SURE... I-I GUESS...
AND YOUR MOM
I ARE VERY PR
OF YOU FOR IT, T

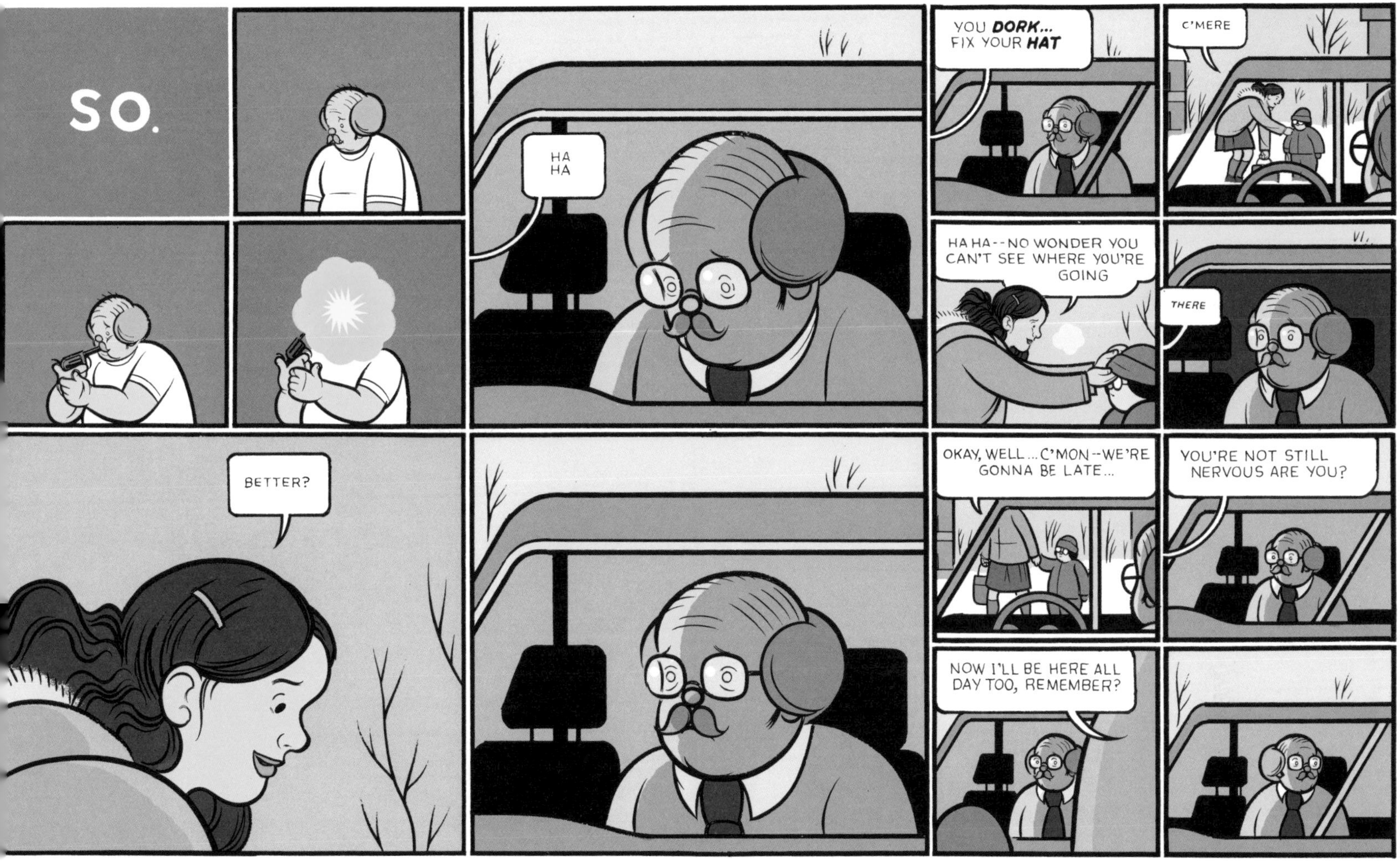
SO.
HA HA
YOU **DORK...** FIX YOUR **HAT**
C'MERE
HA HA--NO WONDER YOU CAN'T SEE WHERE YOU'RE GOING
THERE
BETTER?
OKAY, WELL... C'MON--WE'RE GONNA BE LATE...
YOU'RE NOT STILL NERVOUS ARE YOU?
NOW I'LL BE HERE ALL DAY TOO, REMEMBER?

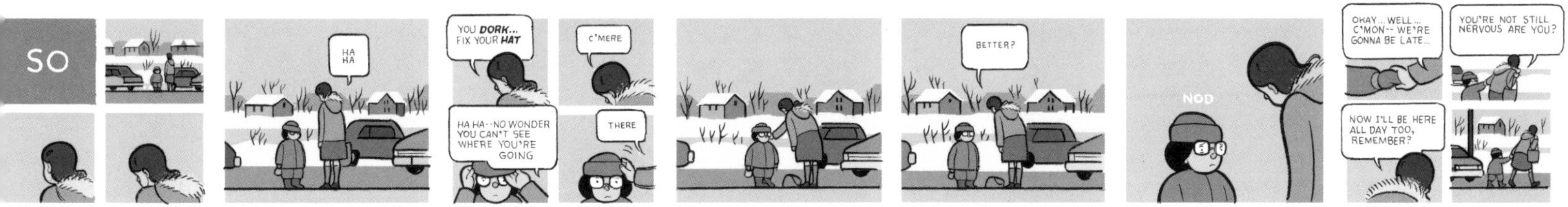
SO
HA HA
YOU **DORK...** FIX YOUR **HAT**
C'MERE
HA HA--NO WONDER YOU CAN'T SEE WHERE YOU'RE GOING
THERE
BETTER?
NOD
OKAY... WELL... C'MON-- WE'RE GONNA BE LATE...
YOU'RE NOT STILL NERVOUS ARE YOU?
NOW I'LL BE HERE ALL DAY TOO, REMEMBER?

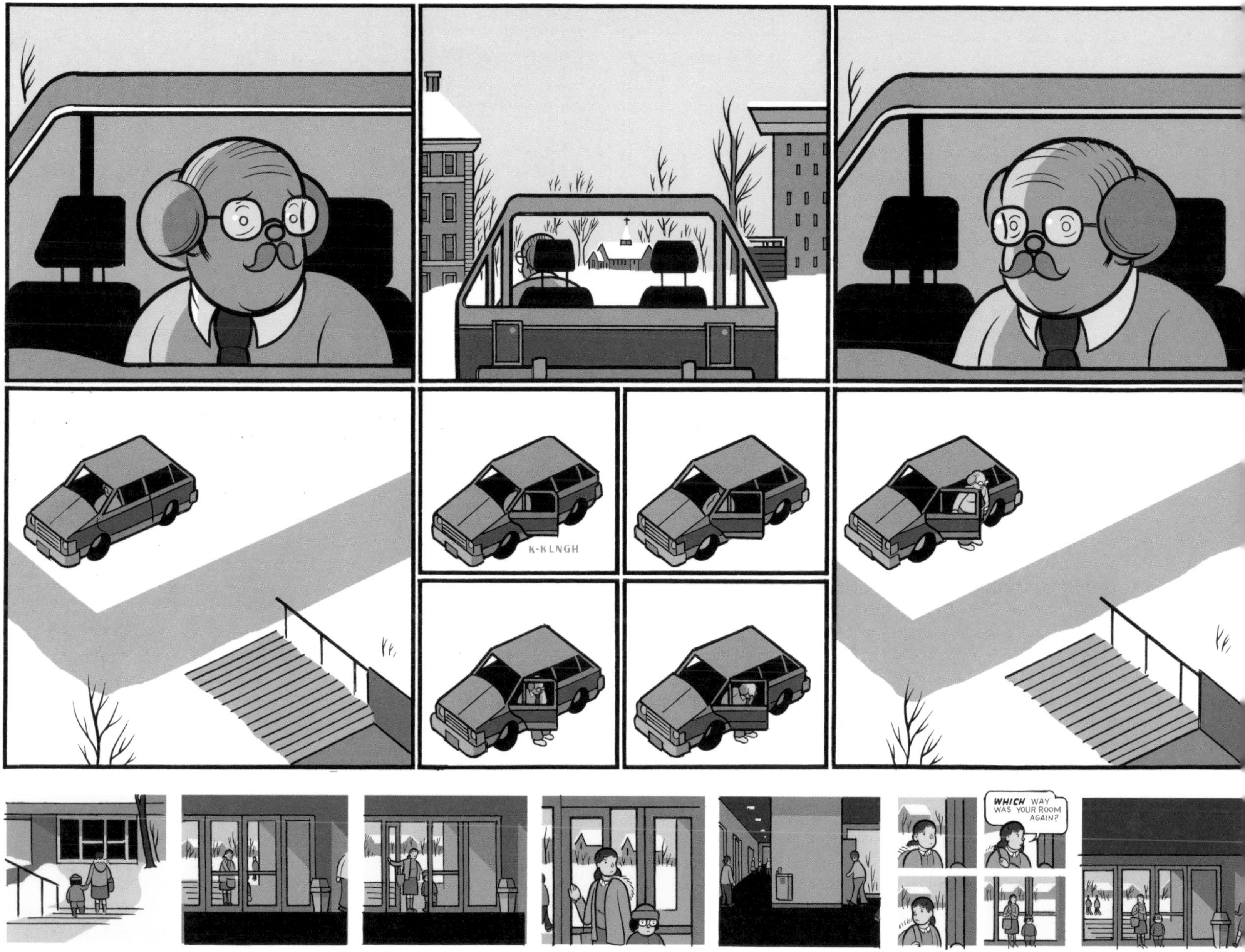
K-KLNGH
WHICH WAY WAS YOUR ROOM AGAIN?

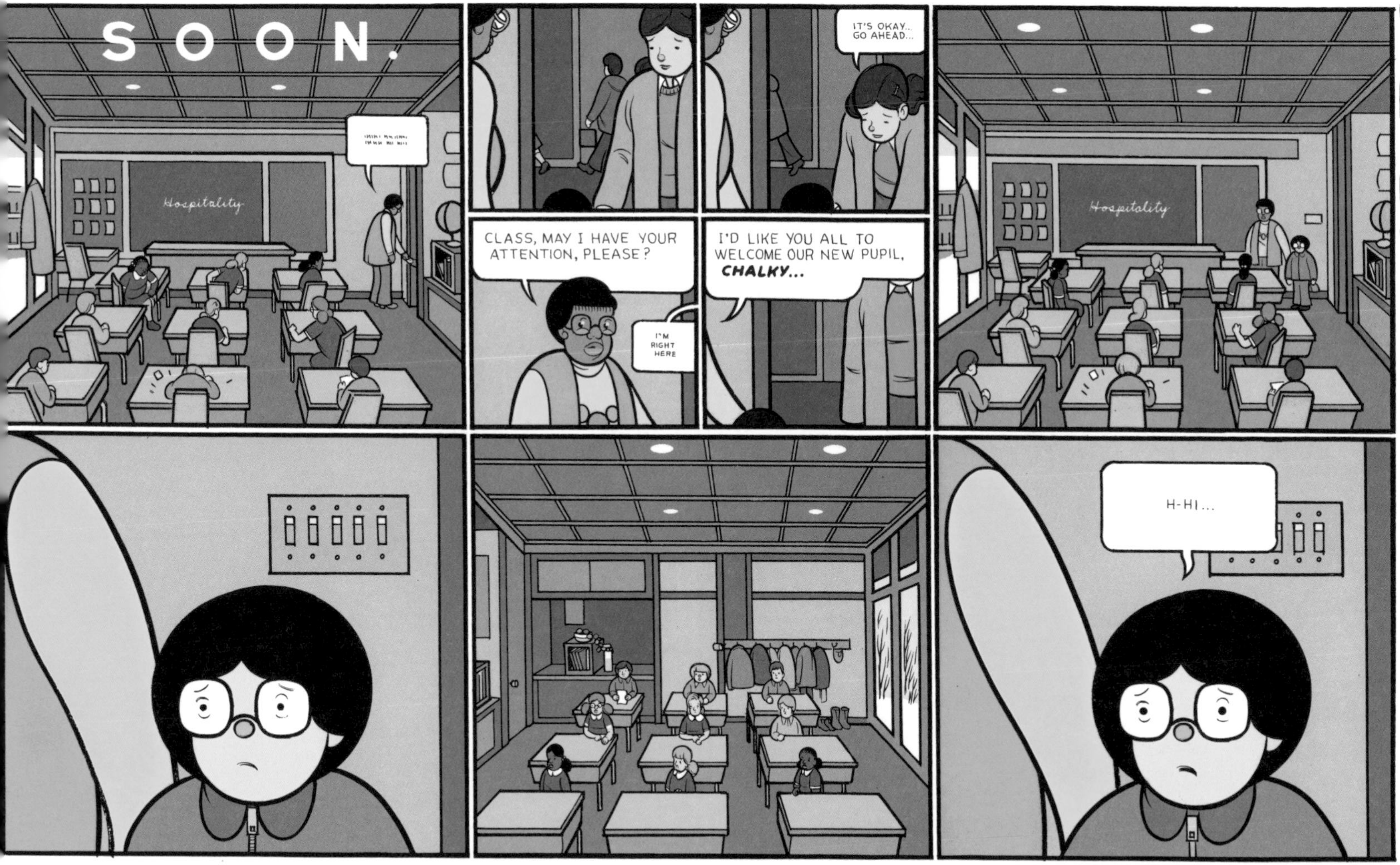
SOON.
IT'S OKAY... GO AHEAD...
CLASS, MAY I HAVE YOUR ATTENTION, PLEASE?
I'M RIGHT HERE
I'D LIKE YOU ALL TO WELCOME OUR NEW PUPIL, CHALKY...
Hospitality
H-HI...

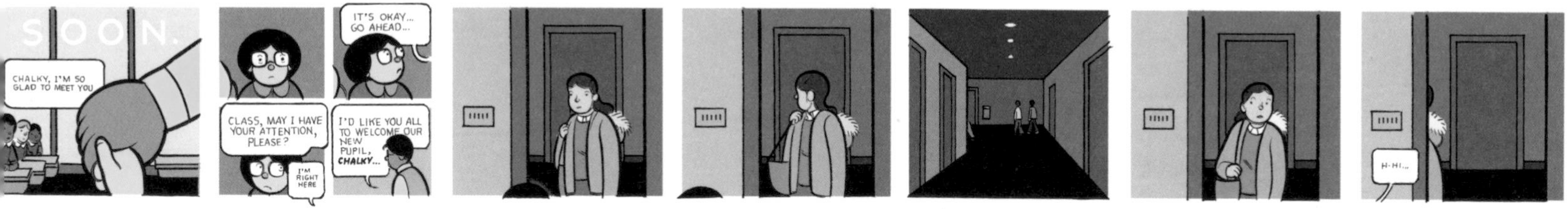
SOON.
CHALKY, I'M SO GLAD TO MEET YOU
IT'S OKAY... GO AHEAD...
CLASS, MAY I HAVE YOUR ATTENTION, PLEASE?
I'M RIGHT HERE
I'D LIKE YOU ALL TO WELCOME OUR NEW PUPIL, CHALKY...
H-HI...

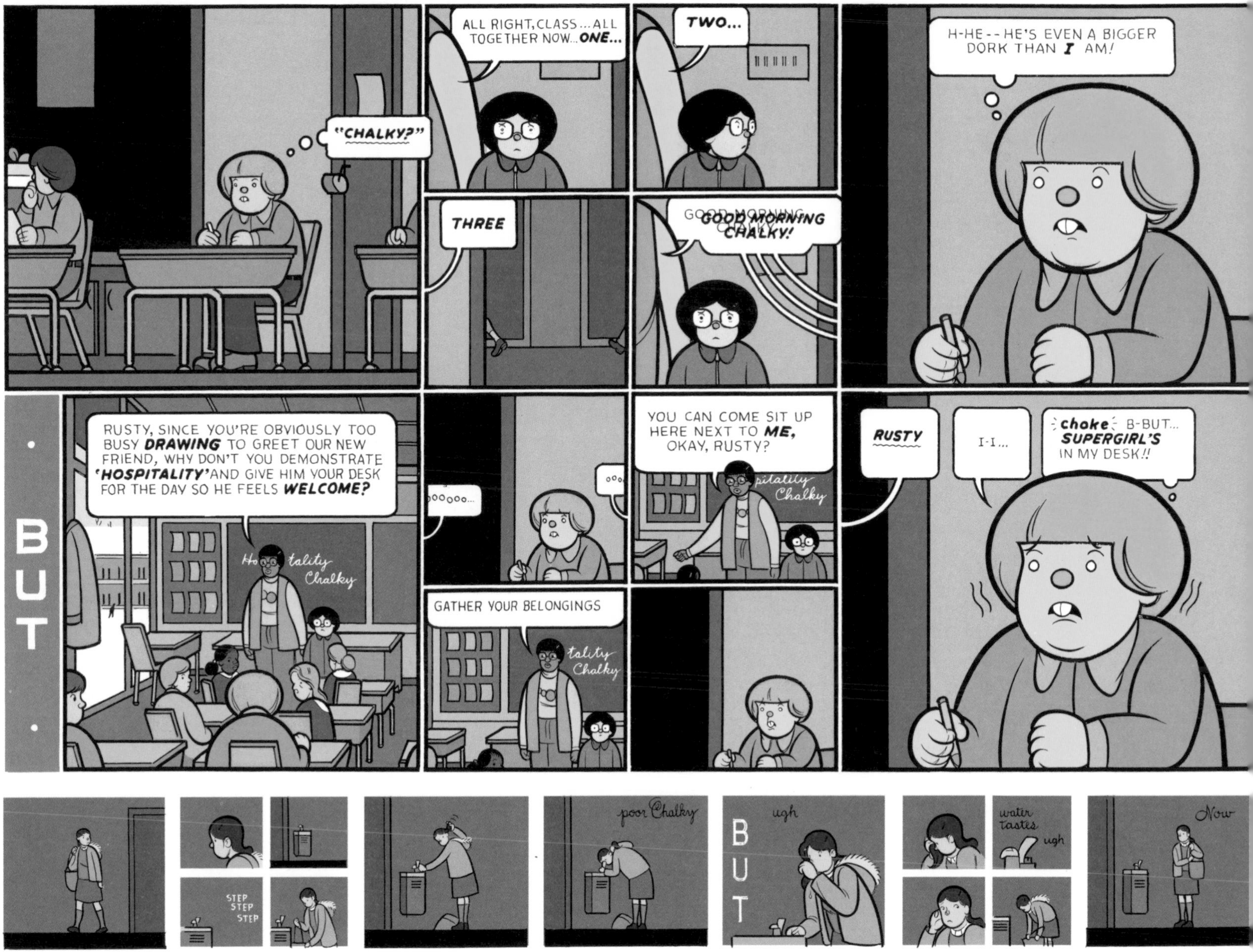
"CHALKY?"
ALL RIGHT, CLASS... ALL TOGETHER NOW... ONE...
TWO...
THREE
GOOD MORNING CHALKY!
H-HE-- HE'S EVEN A BIGGER DORK THAN I AM!
BUT
RUSTY, SINCE YOU'RE OBVIOUSLY TOO BUSY DRAWING TO GREET OUR NEW FRIEND, WHY DON'T YOU DEMONSTRATE 'HOSPITALITY' AND GIVE HIM YOUR DESK FOR THE DAY SO HE FEELS WELCOME?
oooooo...
ooo
GATHER YOUR BELONGINGS
YOU CAN COME SIT UP HERE NEXT TO ME, OKAY, RUSTY?
RUSTY
I-I...
choke B-BUT... SUPERGIRL'S IN MY DESK!!
STEP STEP STEP
poor Chalky
BUT
ugh
water tastes
ugh
Now

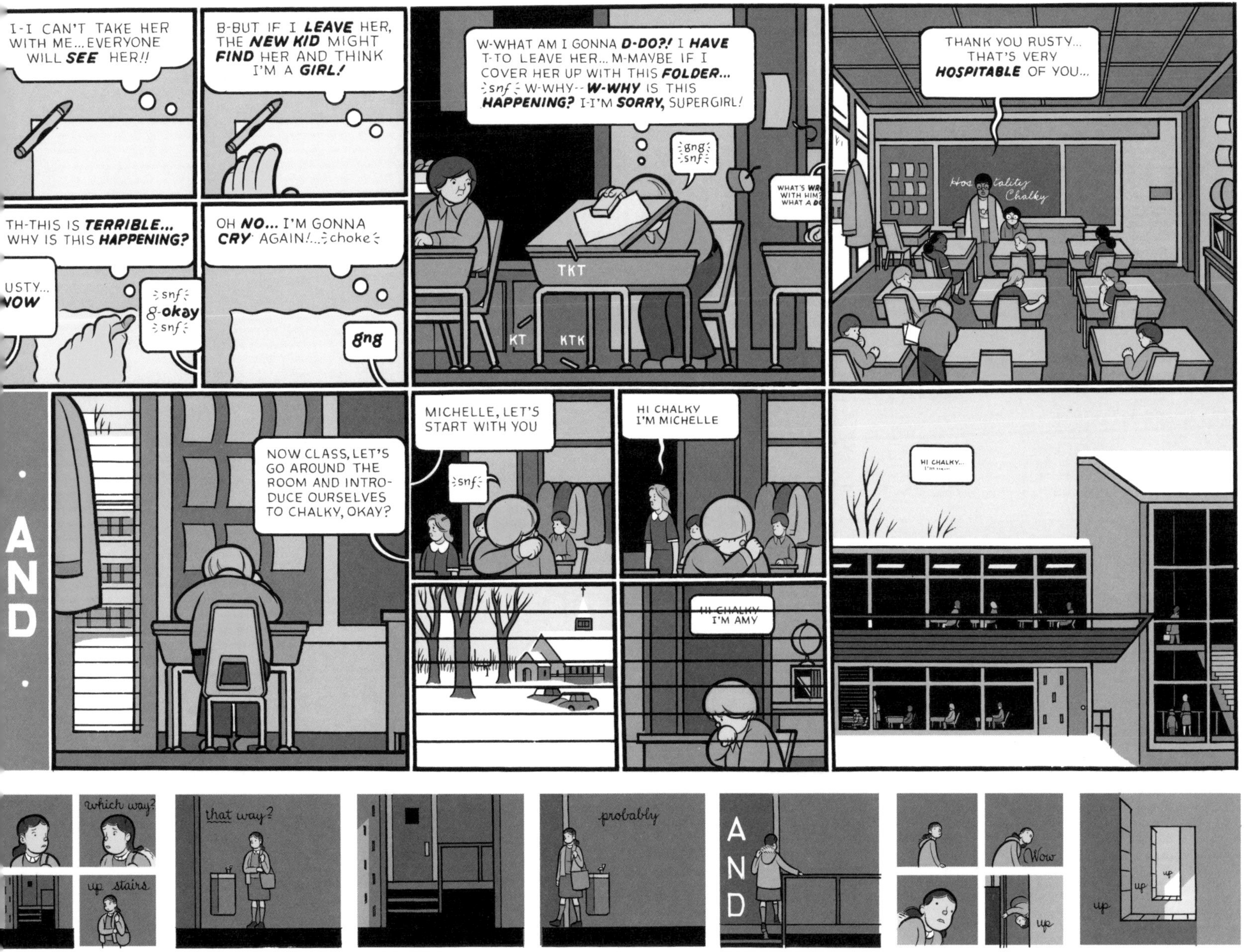
I-I CAN'T TAKE HER WITH ME... EVERYONE WILL SEE HER!!
B-BUT IF I LEAVE HER, THE NEW KID MIGHT FIND HER AND THINK I'M A GIRL!
TH-THIS IS TERRIBLE... WHY IS THIS HAPPENING?
USTY... NOW
snf g-okay snf
OH NO... I'M GONNA CRY AGAIN!... choke
gng
W-WHAT AM I GONNA D-DO?! I HAVE T-TO LEAVE HER... M-MAYBE IF I COVER HER UP WITH THIS FOLDER... snf W-WHY-- W-WHY IS THIS HAPPENING? I-I'M SORRY, SUPERGIRL!
gng snf
WITH HIM?
TKT
KT
KTK
THANK YOU RUSTY... THAT'S VERY HOSPITABLE OF YOU...
Chalky
AND
NOW CLASS, LET'S GO AROUND THE ROOM AND INTRODUCE OURSELVES TO CHALKY, OKAY?
MICHELLE, LET'S START WITH YOU
snf
HI CHALKY I'M MICHELLE
HI CHALKY I'M AMY
HI CHALKY...
which way?
up stairs
that way?
probably
AND
Wow
up
up
up
up

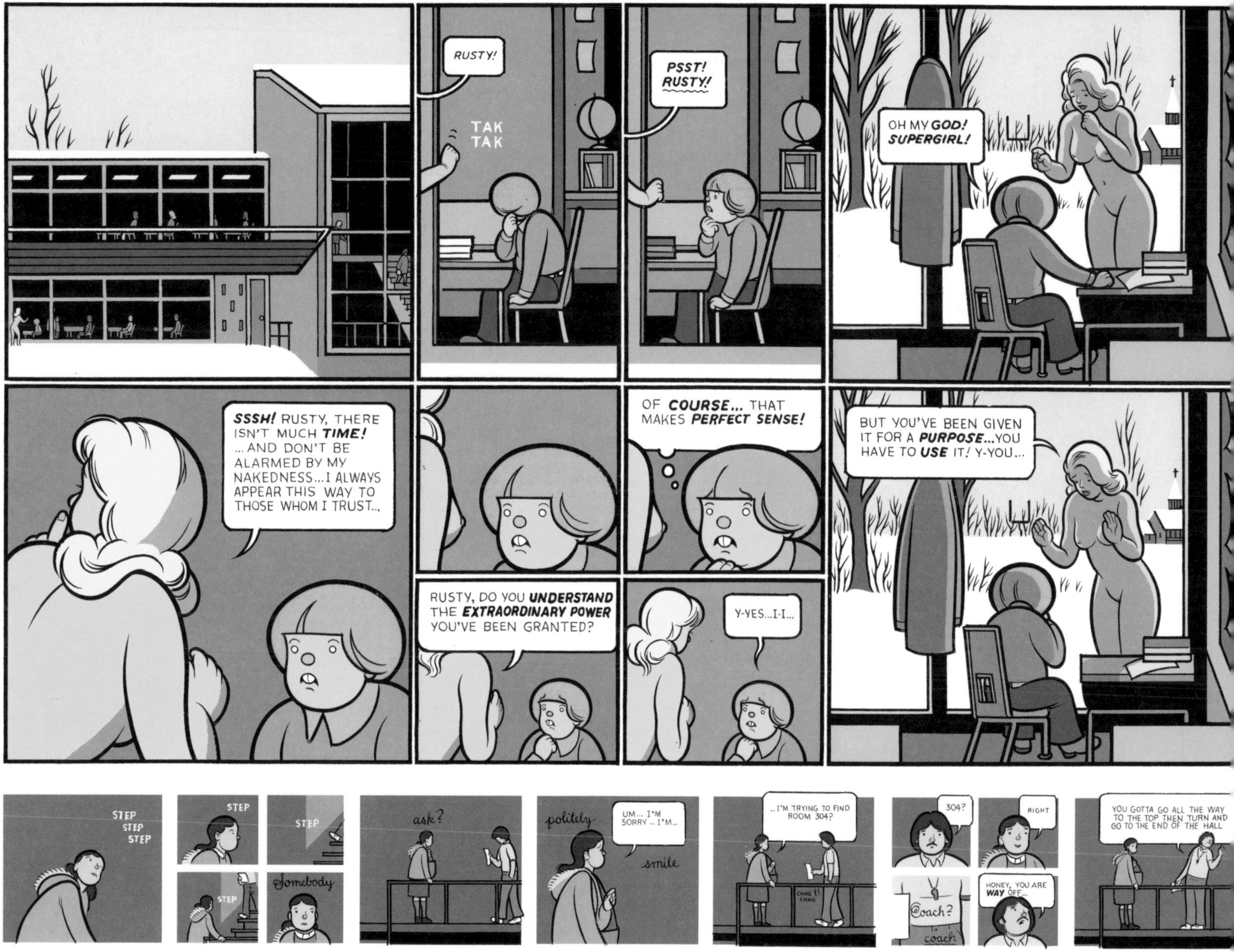
RUSTY!
TAK TAK
PSST! RUSTY!
OH MY GOD! SUPERGIRL!
SSSH! RUSTY, THERE ISN'T MUCH TIME! ...AND DON'T BE ALARMED BY MY NAKEDNESS...I ALWAYS APPEAR THIS WAY TO THOSE WHOM I TRUST...
OF COURSE... THAT MAKES PERFECT SENSE!
RUSTY, DO YOU UNDERSTAND THE EXTRAORDINARY POWER YOU'VE BEEN GRANTED?
Y-YES...I-I...
BUT YOU'VE BEEN GIVEN IT FOR A PURPOSE...YOU HAVE TO USE IT! Y-YOU...
STEP STEP STEP
STEP
STEP
STEP
Somebody
ask?
politely
UM... I'M SORRY ... I'M...
smile
...I'M TRYING TO FIND ROOM 304?
CHNG CHNG
304?
RIGHT
Coach?
coach
HONEY, YOU ARE WAY OFF...
YOU GOTTA GO ALL THE WAY TO THE TOP THEN TURN AND GO TO THE END OF THE HALL

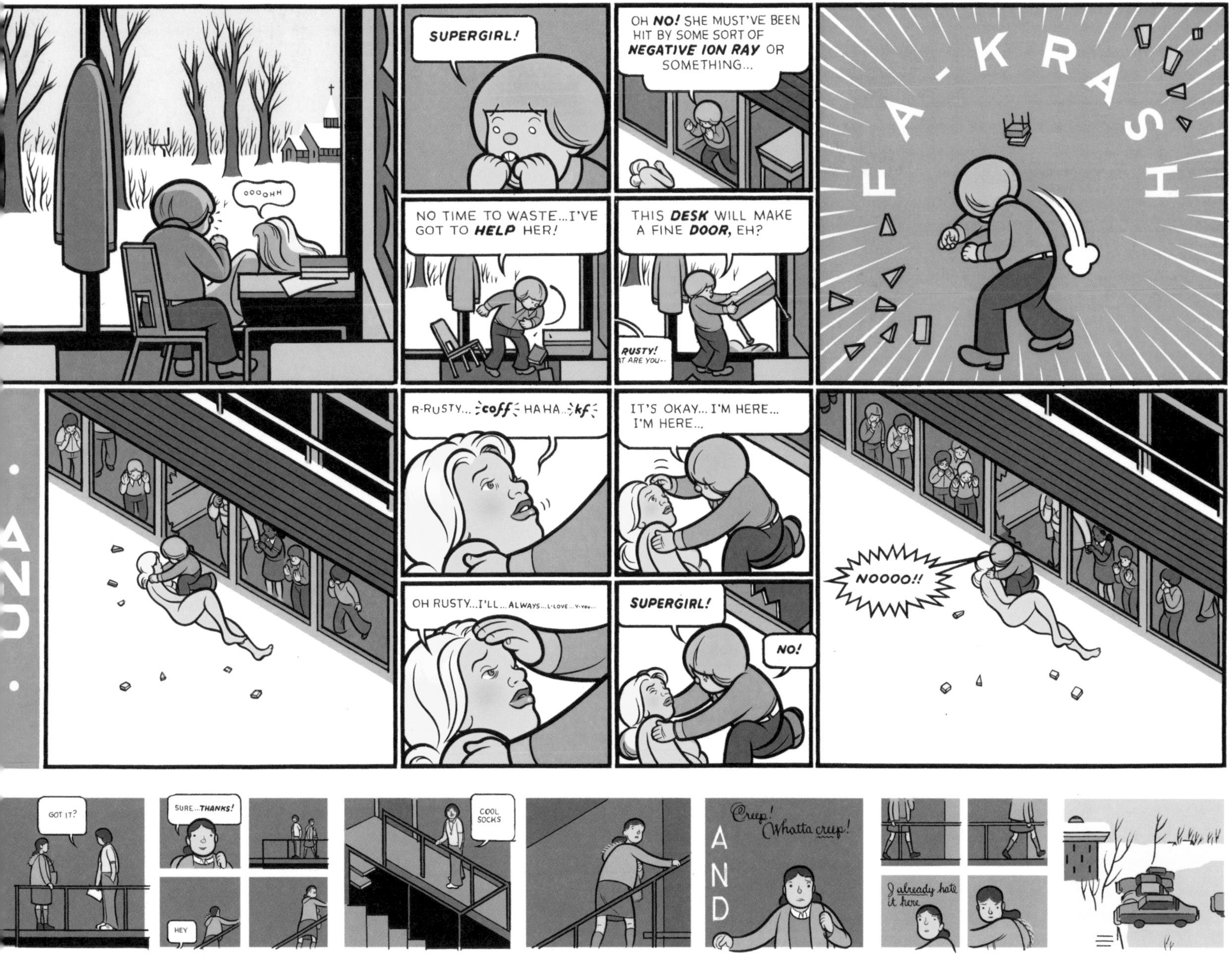
OOOOHH
SUPERGIRL!
OH NO! SHE MUST'VE BEEN HIT BY SOME SORT OF NEGATIVE ION RAY OR SOMETHING...
NO TIME TO WASTE...I'VE GOT TO HELP HER!
THIS DESK WILL MAKE A FINE DOOR, EH?
RUSTY!
FA-KRASH
R-RUSTY... coff HA HA... kf
IT'S OKAY... I'M HERE... I'M HERE...
OH RUSTY...I'LL...ALWAYS...L-LOVE...Y-YOU...
SUPERGIRL!
NO!
NOOOO!!
GOT IT?
SURE...THANKS!
HEY
COOL SOCKS
AND
Creep! Whatta creep!
I already hate it here

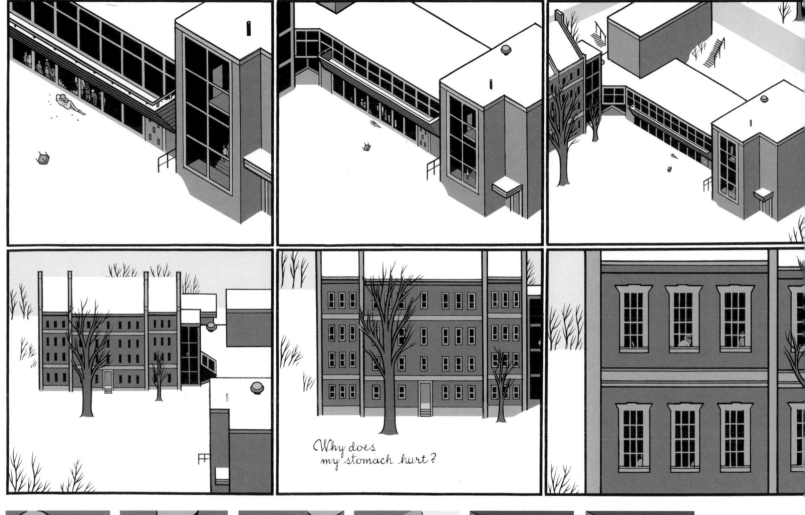

Why does
my stomach hurt?

my stomach
hurts

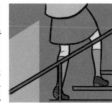

school smell
New school
smell
maybe
makes it hurt
I hate it
hate
hate
hate it
The Who
BLACK SABBATH
EXIT
What is it? floor wax?
late I can't be late fourth floor
fourth floor wax
EXIT
Ugh!
I want to go...
I know
Nobody nobody is going to like me...
EXIT
SHUT
Nobody...
K-GHNK
snf

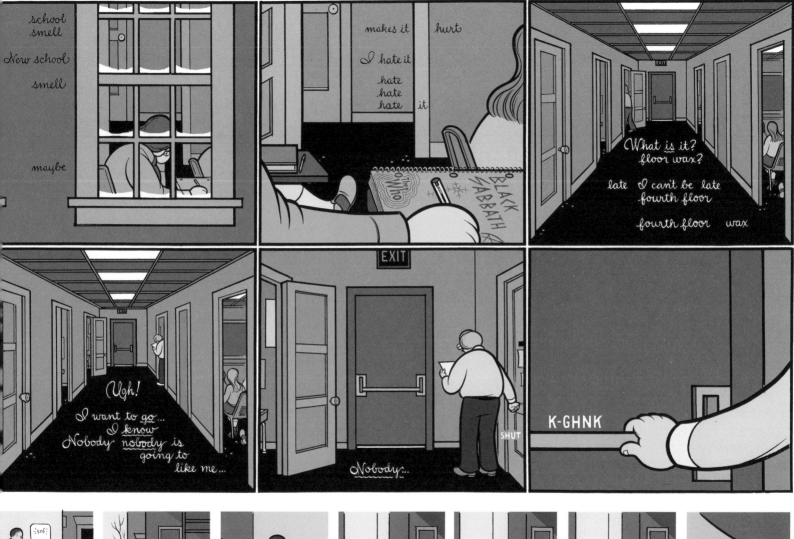

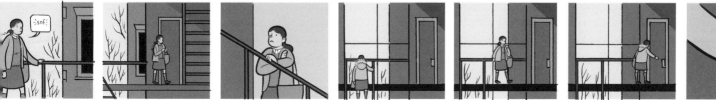

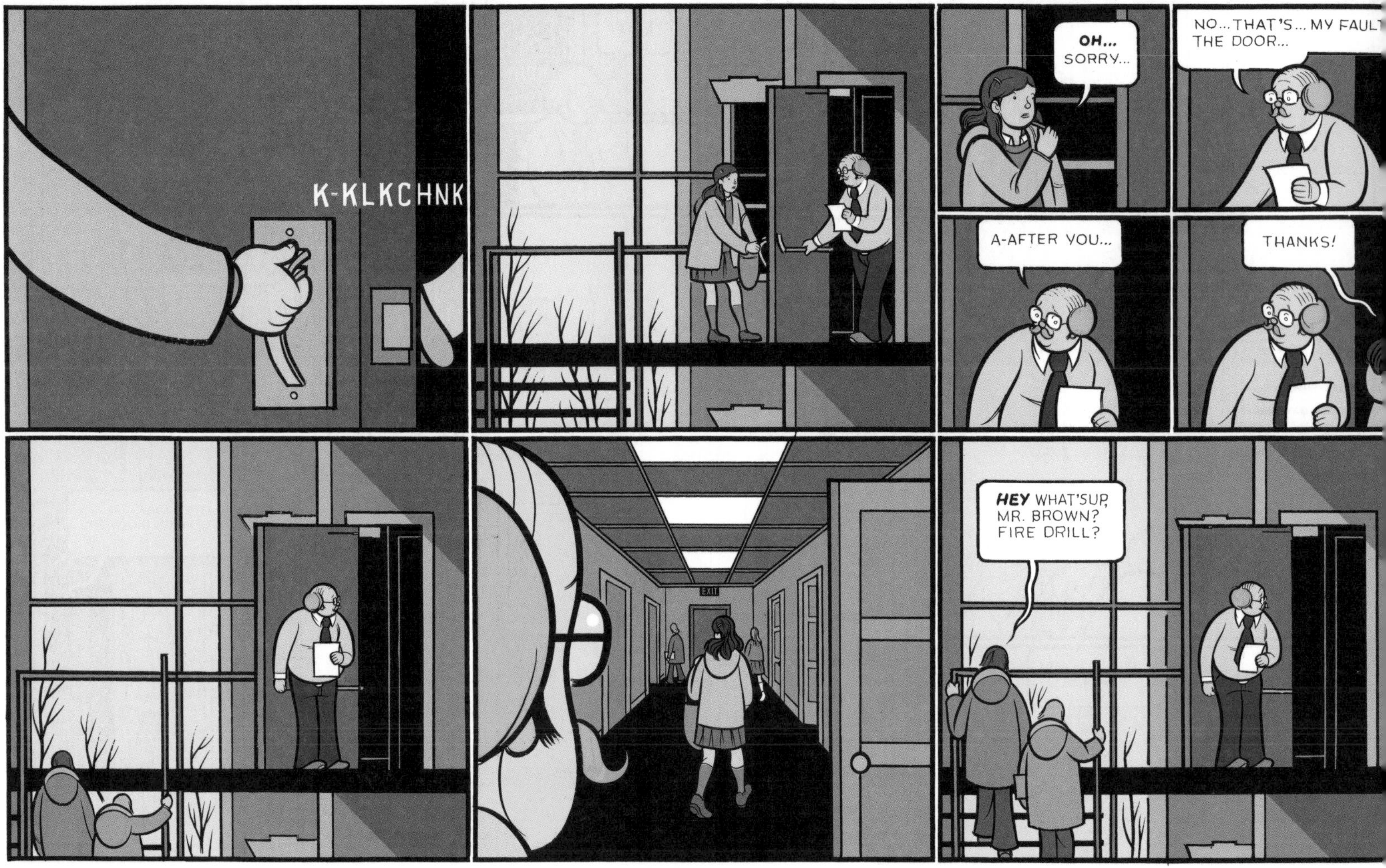
K-KLKCHNK
OH... SORRY...
NO... THAT'S... MY FAUL
THE DOOR...
A-AFTER YOU...
THANKS!
EXIT
HEY WHAT'SUP, MR. BROWN? FIRE DRILL?

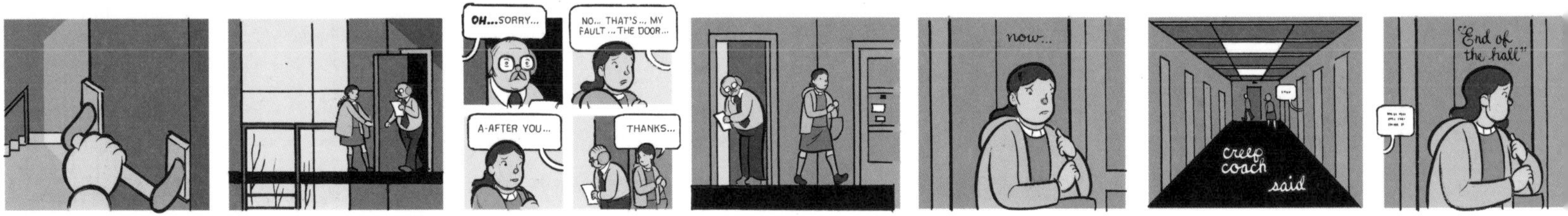
OH... SORRY...
NO... THAT'S... MY FAULT... THE DOOR...
A-AFTER YOU...
THANKS...
now...
creep coach said
"End of the hall"

UH
NO
koff
KCHNK
I CERTAINLY HOPE YOU TWO HAVE DONE YOUR **READING** TODAY, THOUGH...
FLTR
FLT
ANOTHER POP QUIZ? THAT IS **CRUEL** AND **UNUSUAL,** MR. B!
WELL, THEN CONSIDER YOURSELVES 'WARNED'... AND I'D SUGGEST YOU USE THE TIME BEFORE THE BELL TO 'REFRESH' YOUR 'MEMORIES'...
IF YOU'LL EXCUSE ME...
KOFF
MAN, WHATTA **BUMMER...**
COMB
YEAH
J'**YOU** READ IT?
K-KLK
NAH
ME NEITHER... *snf*... HE'S SUCH A FUCKIN DICKWEED...
KOFF
KOFF
YEAH
314
KCHNK
that means
smaller numbers
this way
don't look...
weird
weird weird weird
this place is so weird
I miss you Gretchen

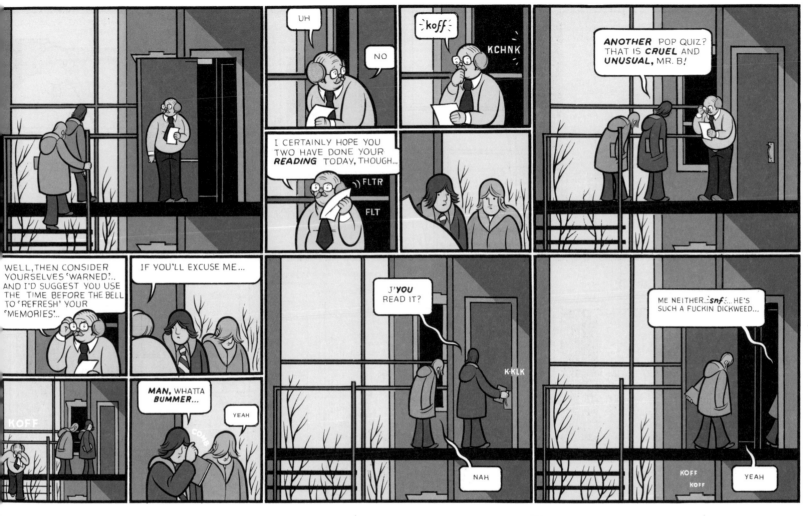

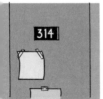

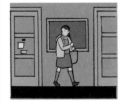

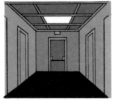

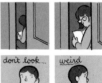

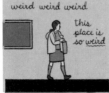

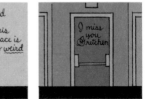

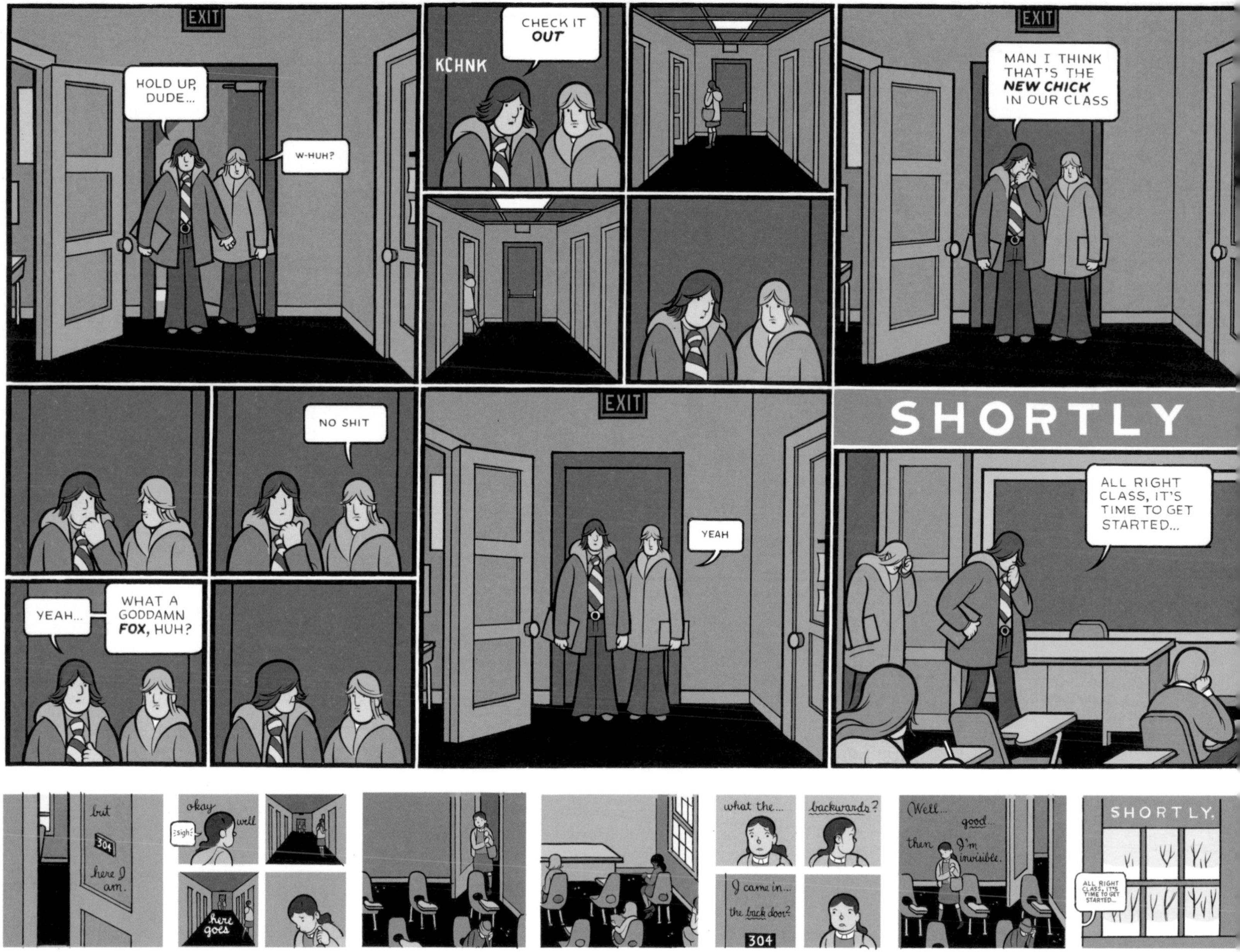
EXIT
HOLD UP, DUDE...
W-HUH?
KCHNK
CHECK IT **OUT**
EXIT
MAN I THINK THAT'S THE **NEW CHICK** IN OUR CLASS
NO SHIT
YEAH...
WHAT A GODDAMN **FOX,** HUH?
EXIT
YEAH
SHORTLY
ALL RIGHT CLASS, IT'S TIME TO GET STARTED...
but
304
here I am.
okay
sigh
well
here goes
what the...
backwards?
I came in... the back door?
304
Well... good... then I'm invisible.
SHORTLY.
ALL RIGHT CLASS, IT'S TIME TO GET STARTED...

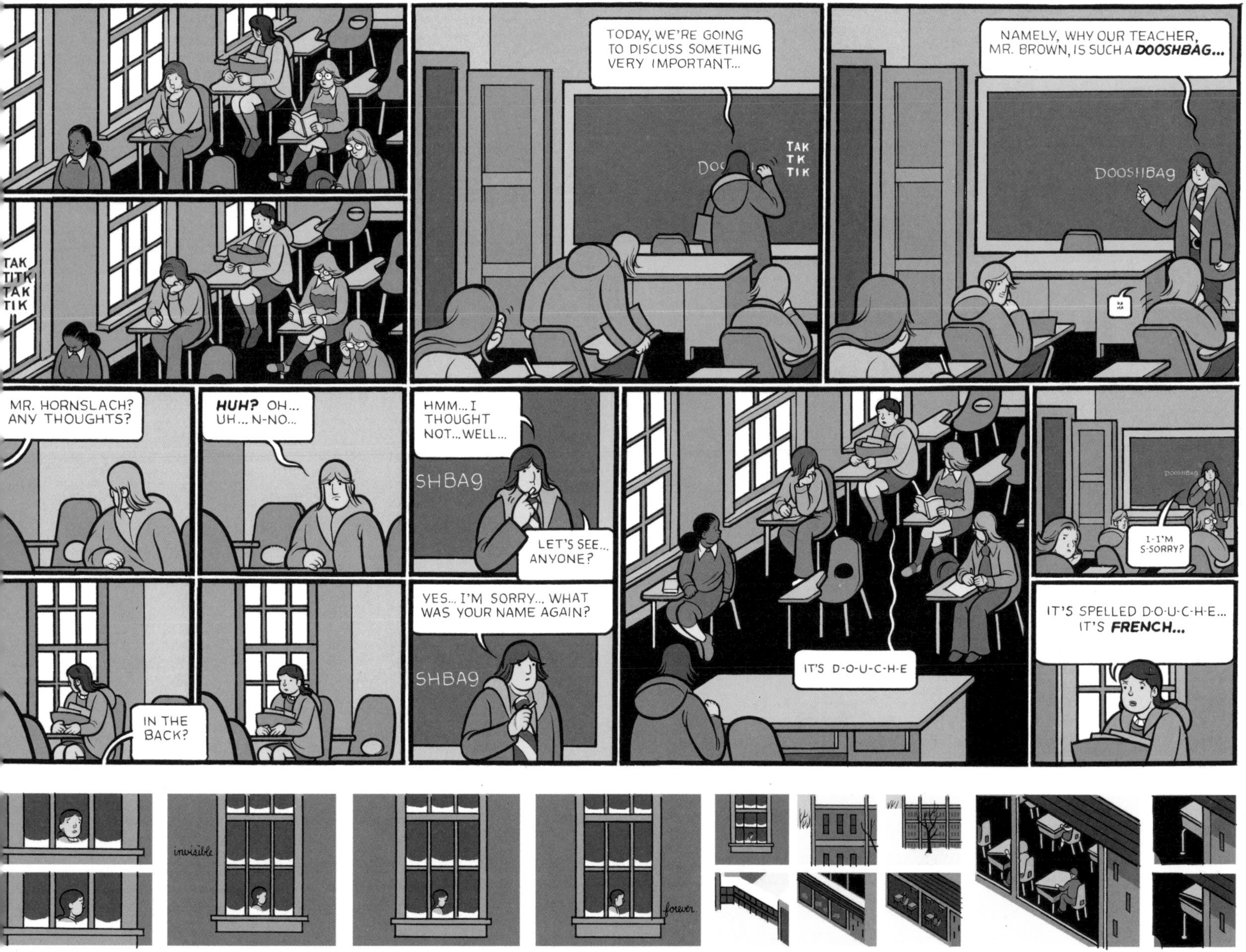

TAK
TITK
TAK
TIK
TODAY, WE'RE GOING TO DISCUSS SOMETHING VERY IMPORTANT...
TAK TK TIK
NAMELY, WHY OUR TEACHER, MR. BROWN, IS SUCH A ***DOOSHBAG...***
DOOSHBAG
MR. HORNSLACH? ANY THOUGHTS?
HUH? OH... UH... N-NO...
IN THE BACK?
HMM... I THOUGHT NOT... WELL...
SHBAG
LET'S SEE... ANYONE?
YES... I'M SORRY... WHAT WAS YOUR NAME AGAIN?
SHBAG
IT'S D-O-U-C-H-E
I-I'M S-SORRY?
IT'S SPELLED D-O-U-C-H-E... IT'S ***FRENCH...***
invisible
forever.

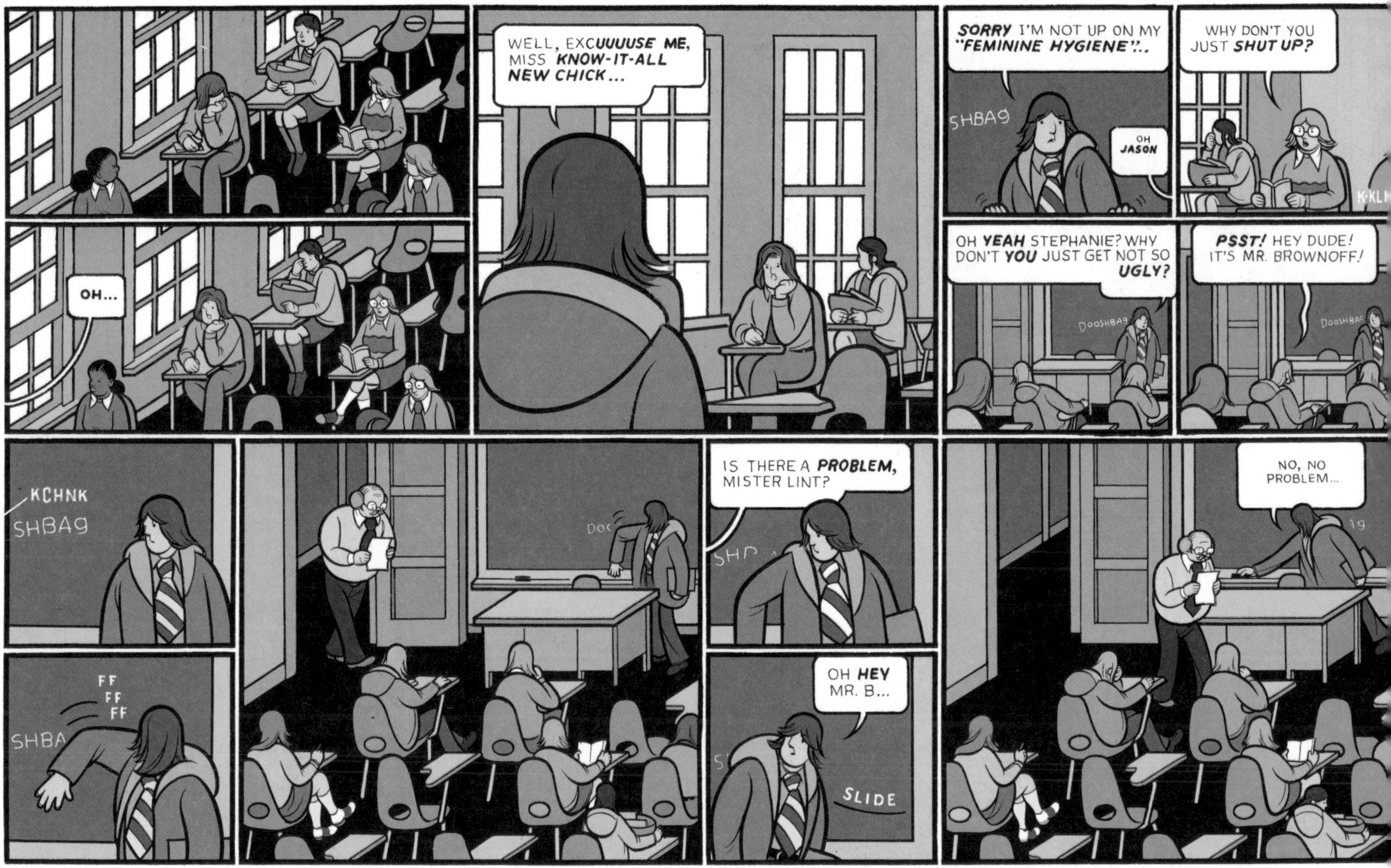
OH...
WELL, EXCUUUUSE ME, MISS KNOW-IT-ALL NEW CHICK...
SORRY I'M NOT UP ON MY "FEMININE HYGIENE"..
SHBAG
OH JASON
WHY DON'T YOU JUST SHUT UP?
OH YEAH STEPHANIE? WHY DON'T YOU JUST GET NOT SO UGLY?
DOOSHBAG
PSST! HEY DUDE! IT'S MR. BROWNOFF!
KCHNK
SHBAG
FF FF FF
SHBA
IS THERE A PROBLEM, MISTER LINT?
OH HEY MR. B...
SLIDE
NO, NO PROBLEM...

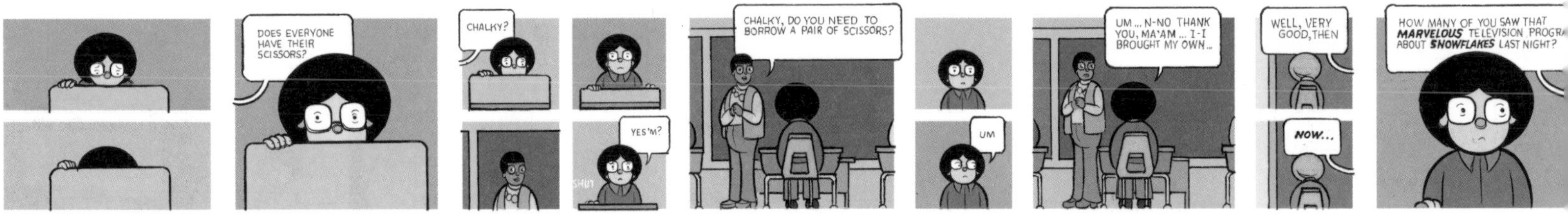
DOES EVERYONE HAVE THEIR SCISSORS?
CHALKY?
YES'M?
CHALKY, DO YOU NEED TO BORROW A PAIR OF SCISSORS?
UM
UM... N-NO THANK YOU, MA'AM... I-I BROUGHT MY OWN...
WELL, VERY GOOD, THEN
NOW...
HOW MANY OF YOU SAW THAT MARVELOUS TELEVISION PROGRA ABOUT SNOWFLAKES LAST NIGHT?

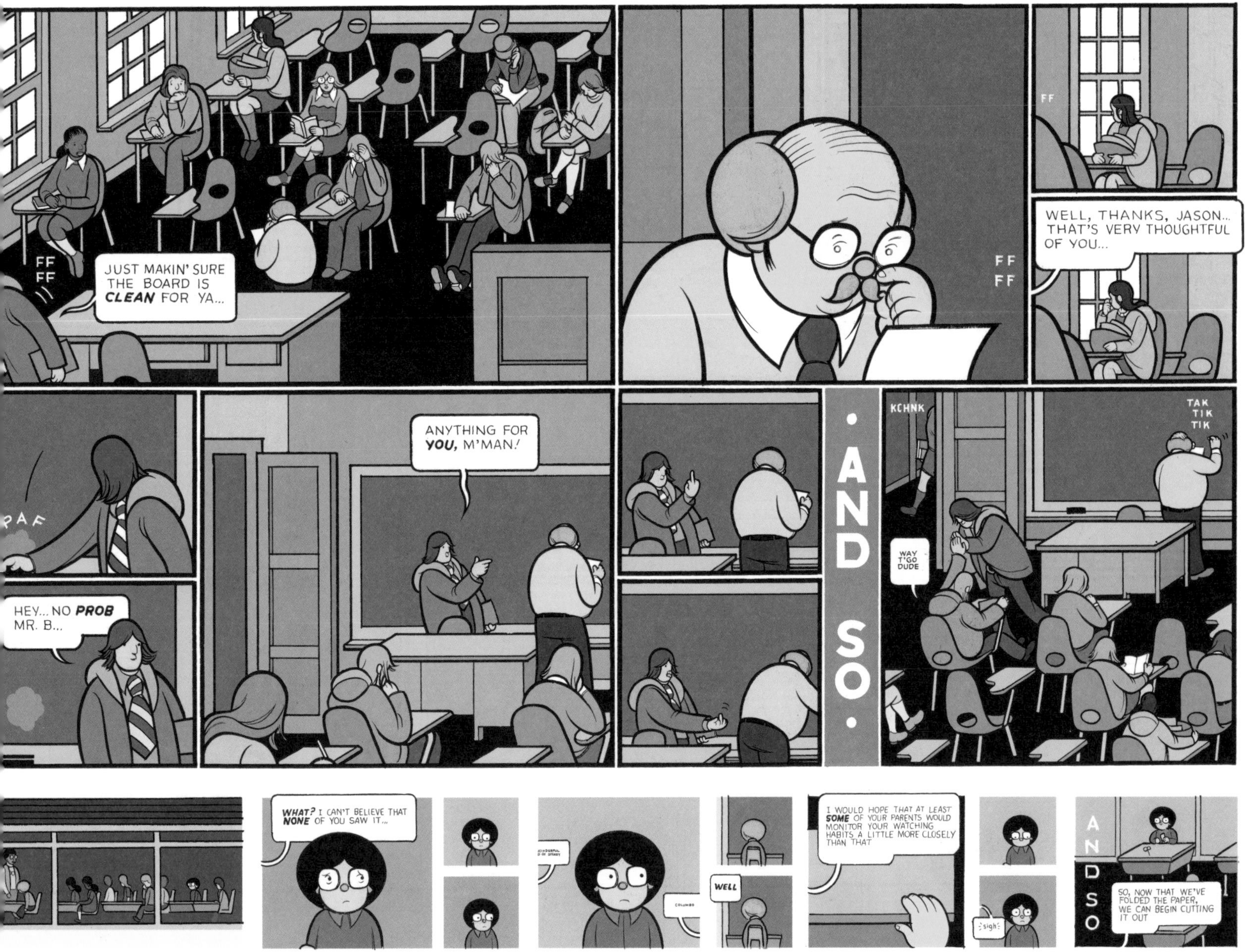
FF
FF
JUST MAKIN' SURE THE BOARD IS **CLEAN** FOR YA...
FF
FF
FF
WELL, THANKS, JASON... THAT'S VERY THOUGHTFUL OF YOU...
PAF
HEY... NO **PROB** MR. B...
ANYTHING FOR **YOU,** M'MAN!
AND SO
KCHNK
TAK
TIK
TIK
WAY T'GO DUDE
WHAT? I CAN'T BELIEVE THAT **NONE** OF YOU SAW IT...
COLUMBO
WELL
I WOULD HOPE THAT AT LEAST **SOME** OF YOUR PARENTS WOULD MONITOR YOUR WATCHING HABITS A LITTLE MORE CLOSELY THAN THAT
sigh
AND SO
SO, NOW THAT WE'VE FOLDED THE PAPER, WE CAN BEGIN CUTTING IT OUT

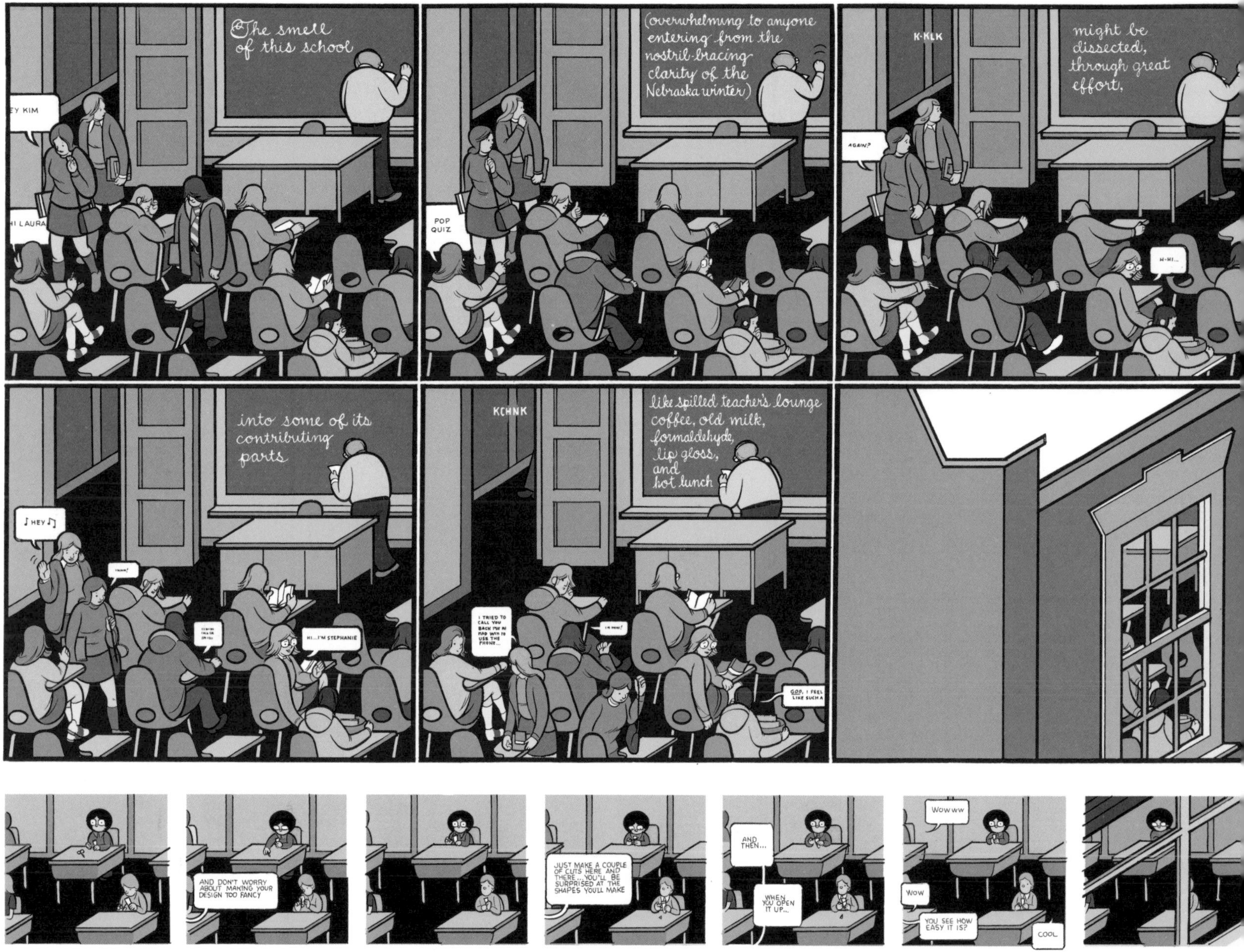
The smell of this school
EY KIM
HI LAURA
(overwhelming to anyone entering from the nostril-bracing clarity of the Nebraska winter)
POP QUIZ
K-KLK
might be dissected, through great effort,
AGAIN?
H-HI...
into some of its contributing parts
♪ HEY ♫
HI...I'M STEPHANIE
KCHNK
like spilled teacher's lounge coffee, old milk, formaldehyde, lip gloss, and hot lunch
I TRIED TO CALL YOU BACK
USE THE PHONE...
GOD, I FEEL LIKE SUCH A
AND DON'T WORRY ABOUT MAKING YOUR DESIGN TOO FANCY
JUST MAKE A COUPLE OF CUTS HERE AND THERE... YOU'LL BE SURPRISED AT THE SHAPES YOU'LL MAKE
AND THEN...
WHEN YOU OPEN IT UP...
Wowww
Wow
YOU SEE HOW EASY IT IS?
COOL

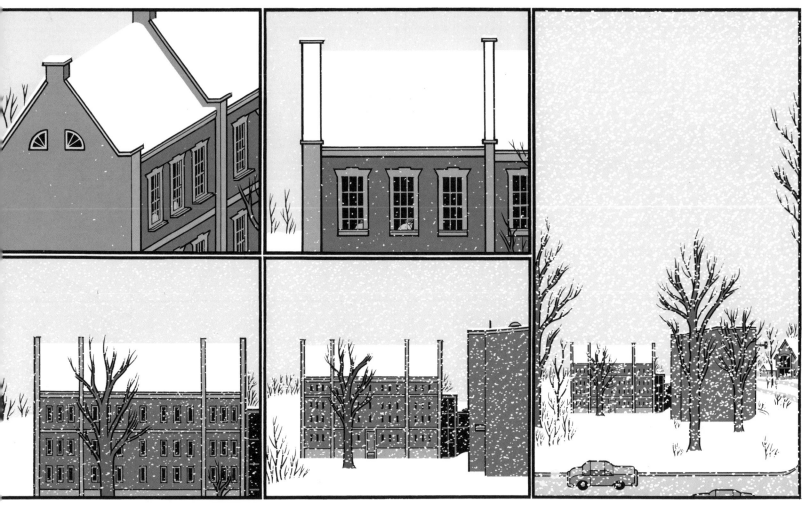

But pinpointing the precise origin of any one of these components

would eventually prove only about as useful

as the successful extraction

of the internal organs of a live frog, pinned into paraffin

gasping

and pleading for its life.

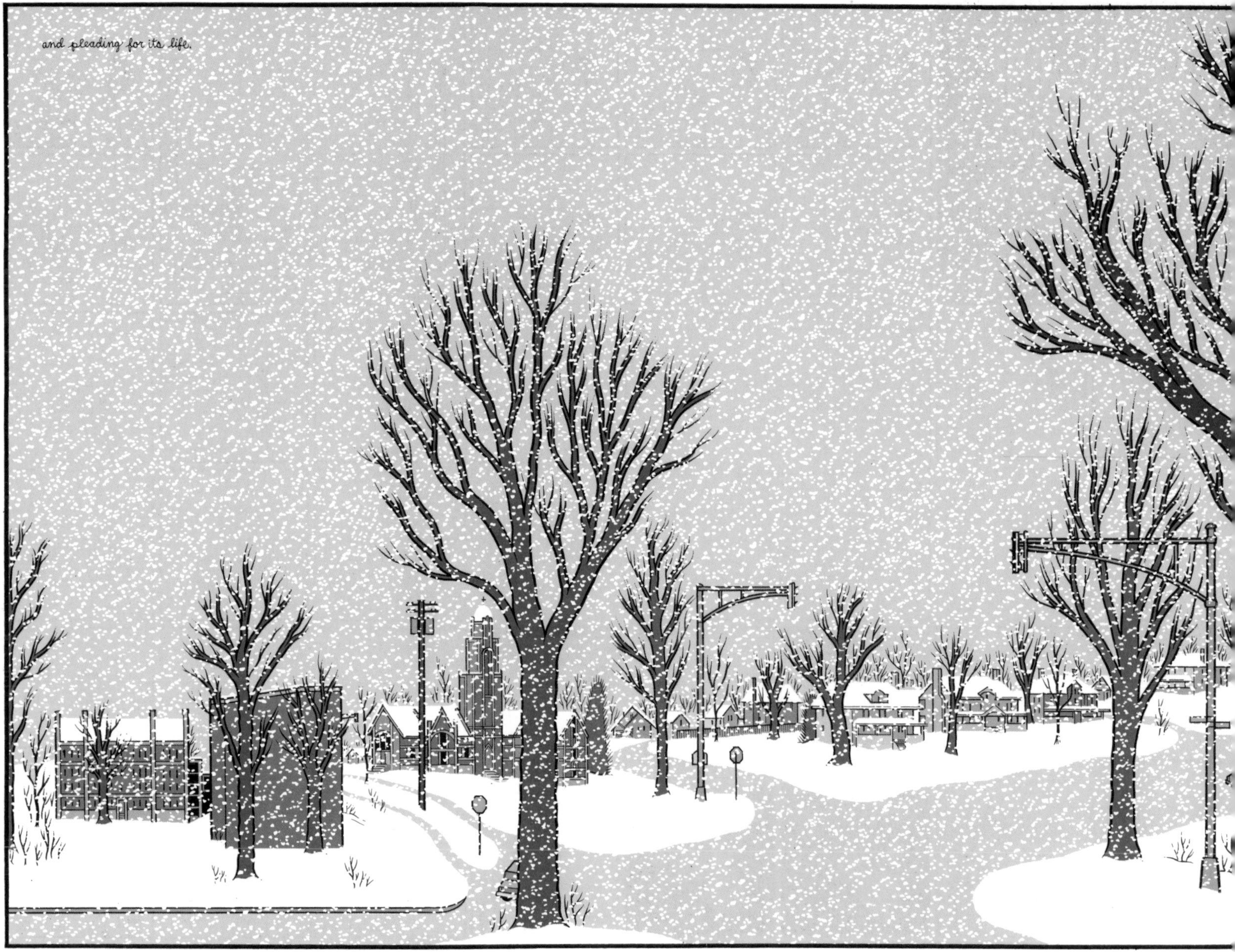

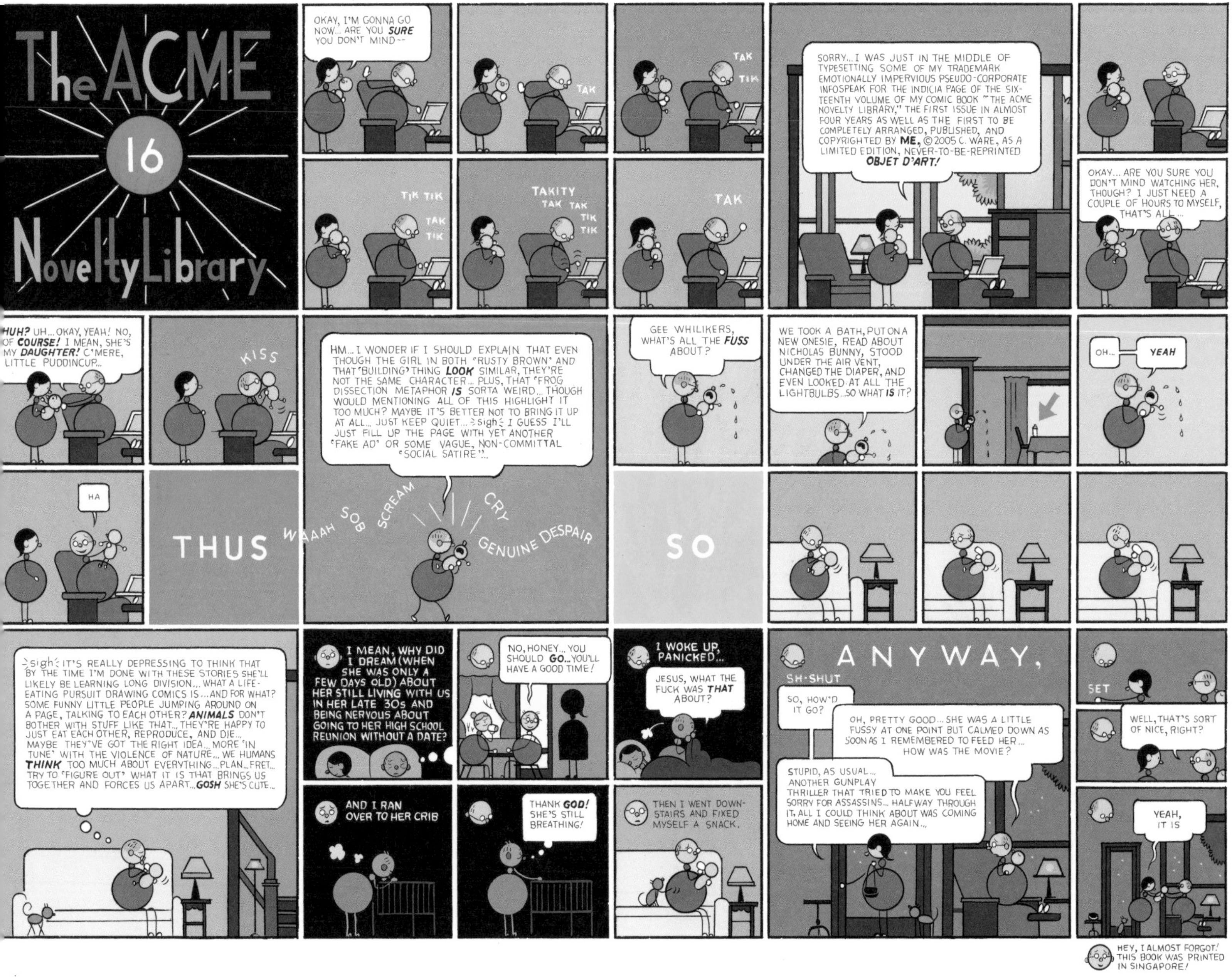
The ACME Novelty Library
16
OKAY, I'M GONNA GO NOW... ARE YOU SURE YOU DON'T MIND--
TAK
TAK
TIK
TIK TIK
TAK
TIK
TAKITY
TAK TAK
TIK
TIK
TAK
SORRY... I WAS JUST IN THE MIDDLE OF TYPESETTING SOME OF MY TRADEMARK EMOTIONALLY IMPERVIOUS PSEUDO-CORPORATE INFOSPEAK FOR THE INDICIA PAGE OF THE SIXTEENTH VOLUME OF MY COMIC BOOK "THE ACME NOVELTY LIBRARY," THE FIRST ISSUE IN ALMOST FOUR YEARS AS WELL AS THE FIRST TO BE COMPLETELY ARRANGED, PUBLISHED, AND COPYRIGHTED BY ME, © 2005 C. WARE, AS A LIMITED EDITION, NEVER-TO-BE-REPRINTED OBJET D'ART!
OKAY... ARE YOU SURE YOU DON'T MIND WATCHING HER, THOUGH? I JUST NEED A COUPLE OF HOURS TO MYSELF, THAT'S ALL...
HUH? UH... OKAY, YEAH! NO, OF COURSE! I MEAN, SHE'S MY DAUGHTER! C'MERE, LITTLE PUDDINCUP...
KISS
HM... I WONDER IF I SHOULD EXPLAIN THAT EVEN THOUGH THE GIRL IN BOTH "RUSTY BROWN" AND THAT "BUILDING" THING LOOK SIMILAR, THEY'RE NOT THE SAME CHARACTER... PLUS, THAT "FROG DISSECTION METAPHOR IS SORTA WEIRD... THOUGH WOULD MENTIONING ALL OF THIS HIGHLIGHT IT TOO MUCH? MAYBE IT'S BETTER NOT TO BRING IT UP AT ALL... JUST KEEP QUIET... ≷sigh≶ I GUESS I'LL JUST FILL UP THE PAGE WITH YET ANOTHER "FAKE AD" OR SOME VAGUE, NON-COMMITTAL "SOCIAL SATIRE"...
GEE WHILIKERS, WHAT'S ALL THE FUSS ABOUT?
WE TOOK A BATH, PUT ON A NEW ONESIE, READ ABOUT NICHOLAS BUNNY, STOOD UNDER THE AIR VENT, CHANGED THE DIAPER, AND EVEN LOOKED AT ALL THE LIGHTBULBS... SO WHAT IS IT?
OH...
YEAH
HA
THUS
WAAAH SOB SCREAM CRY GENUINE DESPAIR
SO
≷sigh≶ IT'S REALLY DEPRESSING TO THINK THAT BY THE TIME I'M DONE WITH THESE STORIES SHE'LL LIKELY BE LEARNING LONG DIVISION... WHAT A LIFE-EATING PURSUIT DRAWING COMICS IS... AND FOR WHAT? SOME FUNNY LITTLE PEOPLE JUMPING AROUND ON A PAGE, TALKING TO EACH OTHER? ANIMALS DON'T BOTHER WITH STUFF LIKE THAT... THEY'RE HAPPY TO JUST EAT EACH OTHER, REPRODUCE, AND DIE... MAYBE THEY'VE GOT THE RIGHT IDEA... MORE "IN TUNE" WITH THE VIOLENCE OF NATURE... WE HUMANS THINK TOO MUCH ABOUT EVERYTHING... PLAN... FRET... TRY TO "FIGURE OUT" WHAT IT IS THAT BRINGS US TOGETHER AND FORCES US APART... GOSH SHE'S CUTE...
I MEAN, WHY DID I DREAM (WHEN SHE WAS ONLY A FEW DAYS OLD) ABOUT HER STILL LIVING WITH US IN HER LATE 30s AND BEING NERVOUS ABOUT GOING TO HER HIGH SCHOOL REUNION WITHOUT A DATE?
NO, HONEY... YOU SHOULD GO... YOU'LL HAVE A GOOD TIME!
I WOKE UP, PANICKED...
JESUS, WHAT THE FUCK WAS THAT ABOUT?
AND I RAN OVER TO HER CRIB
THANK GOD! SHE'S STILL BREATHING!
THEN I WENT DOWNSTAIRS AND FIXED MYSELF A SNACK.
ANYWAY,
SH-SHUT
SO, HOW'D IT GO?
OH, PRETTY GOOD... SHE WAS A LITTLE FUSSY AT ONE POINT BUT CALMED DOWN AS SOON AS I REMEMBERED TO FEED HER... HOW WAS THE MOVIE?
STUPID, AS USUAL... ANOTHER GUNPLAY THRILLER THAT TRIED TO MAKE YOU FEEL SORRY FOR ASSASSINS... HALFWAY THROUGH IT, ALL I COULD THINK ABOUT WAS COMING HOME AND SEEING HER AGAIN...
SET
WELL, THAT'S SORT OF NICE, RIGHT?
YEAH, IT IS
HEY, I ALMOST FORGOT! THIS BOOK WAS PRINTED IN SINGAPORE!

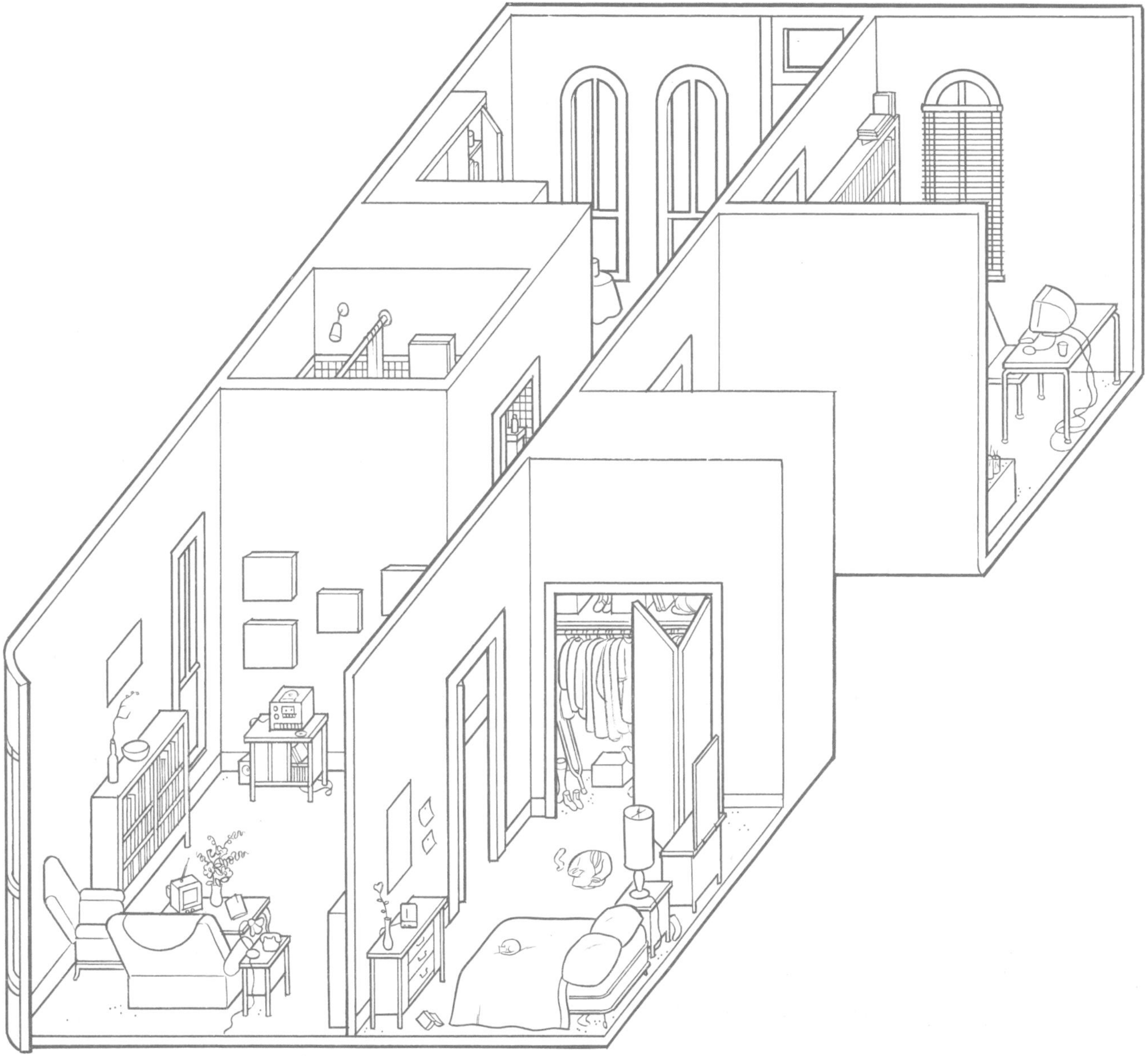

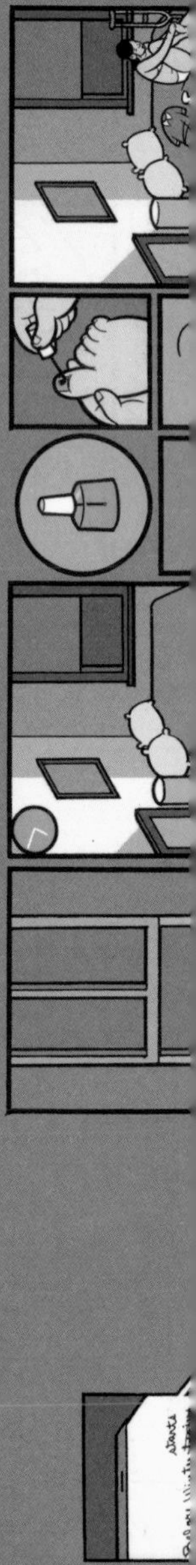

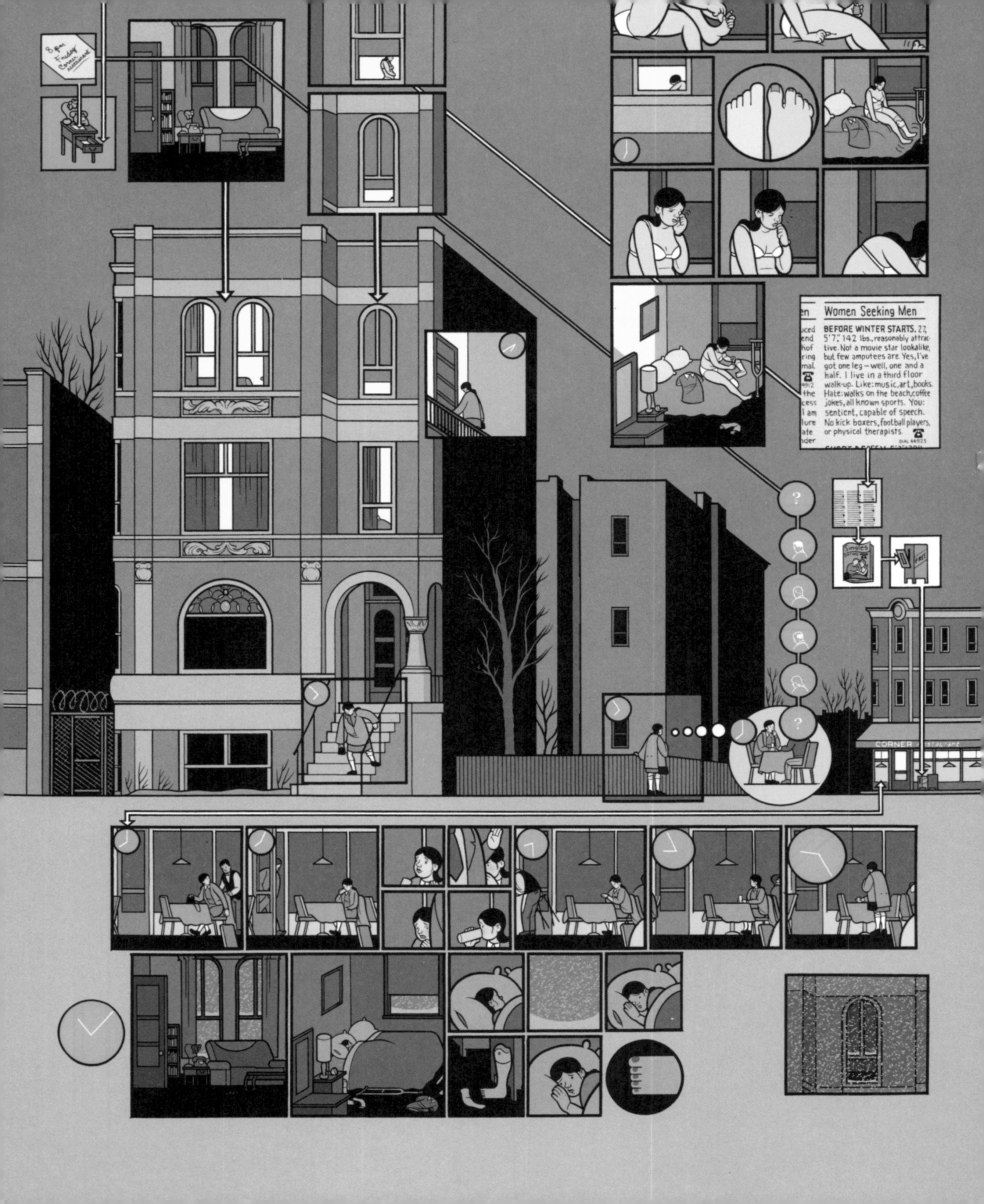
8 pm
Friday
Corner
Restaurant
Women Seeking Men
BEFORE WINTER STARTS. 27, 5'7", 142 lbs., reasonably attractive. Not a movie star lookalike, but few amputees are. Yes, I've got one leg – well, one and a half. I live in a third floor walk-up. Like: music, art, books. Hate: walks on the beach, coffee jokes, all known sports. You: sentient, capable of speech. No kick boxers, football players, or physical therapists.
DIAL 44923
Singles
FREE
?
?
CORNER Restaurant

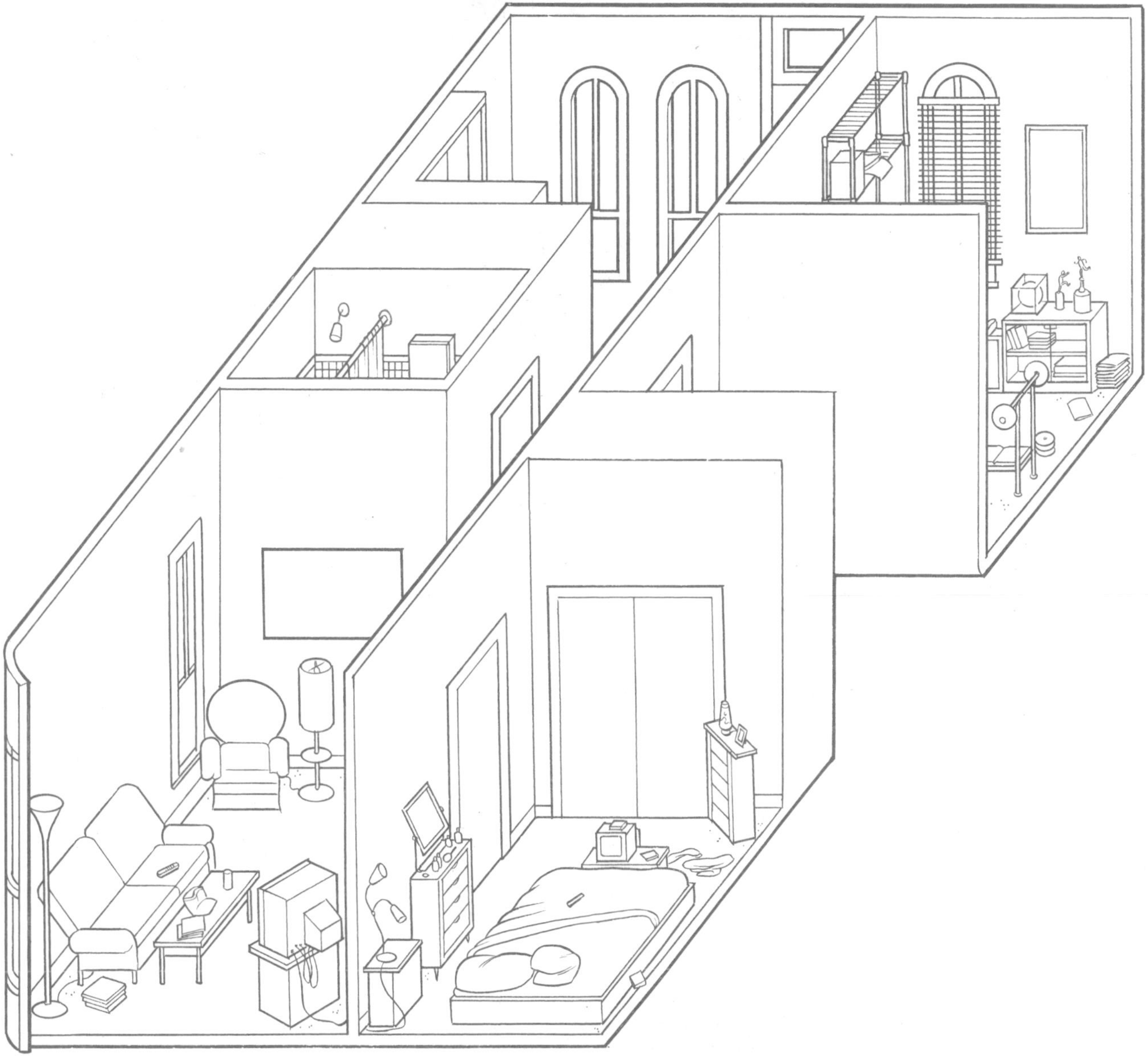

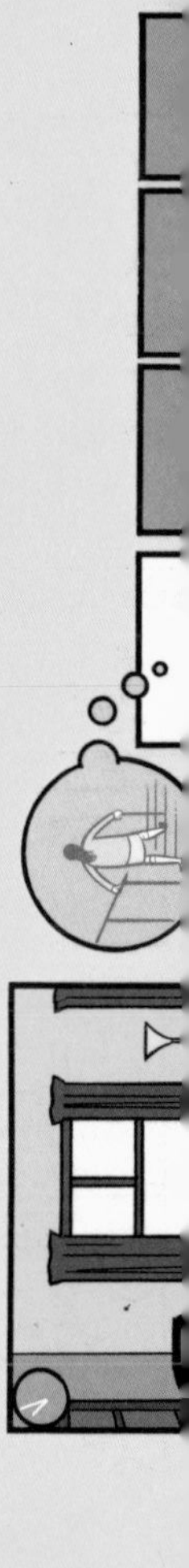

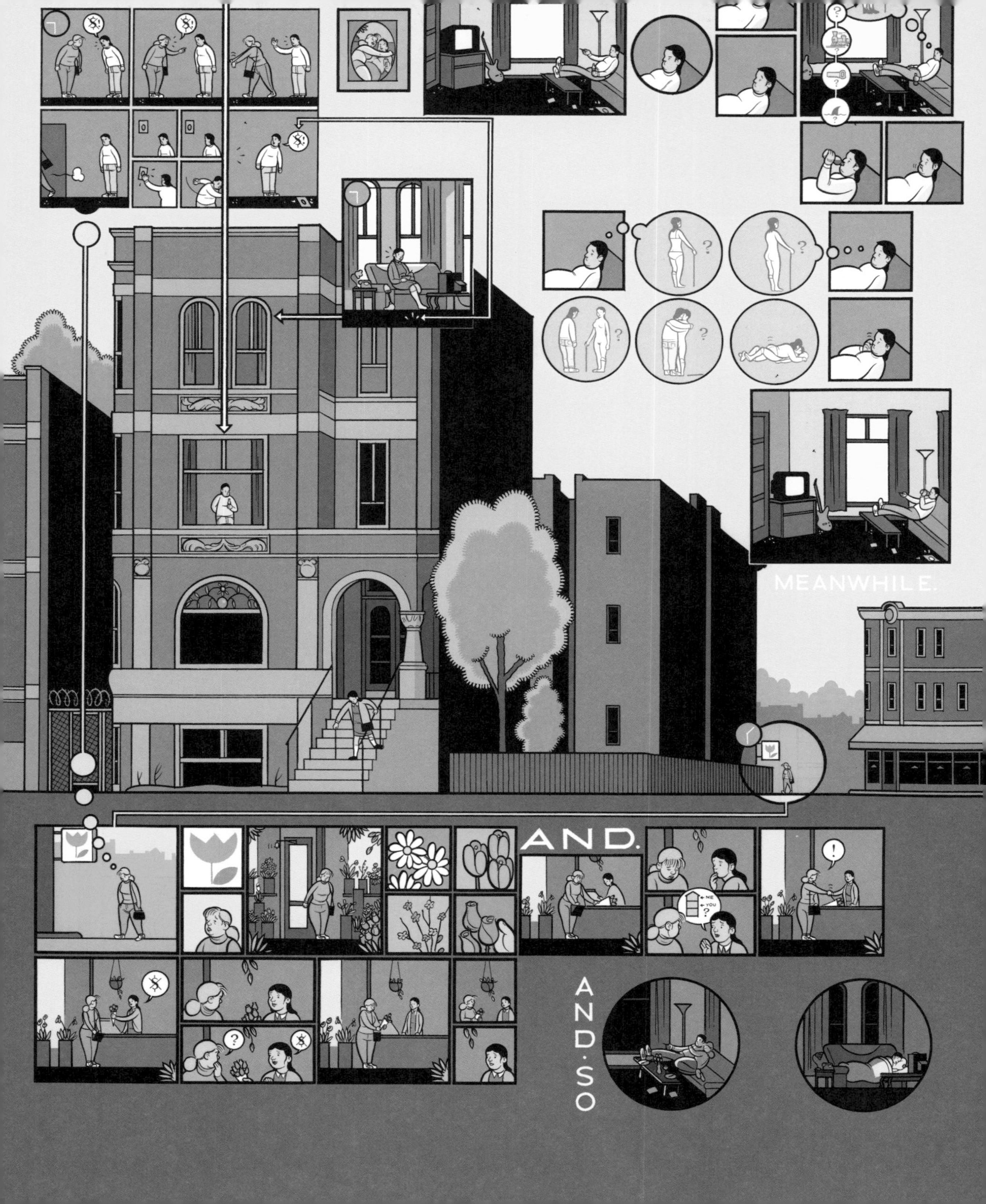
MEANWHILE.
AND.
← ME
← YOU
?
AND·SO

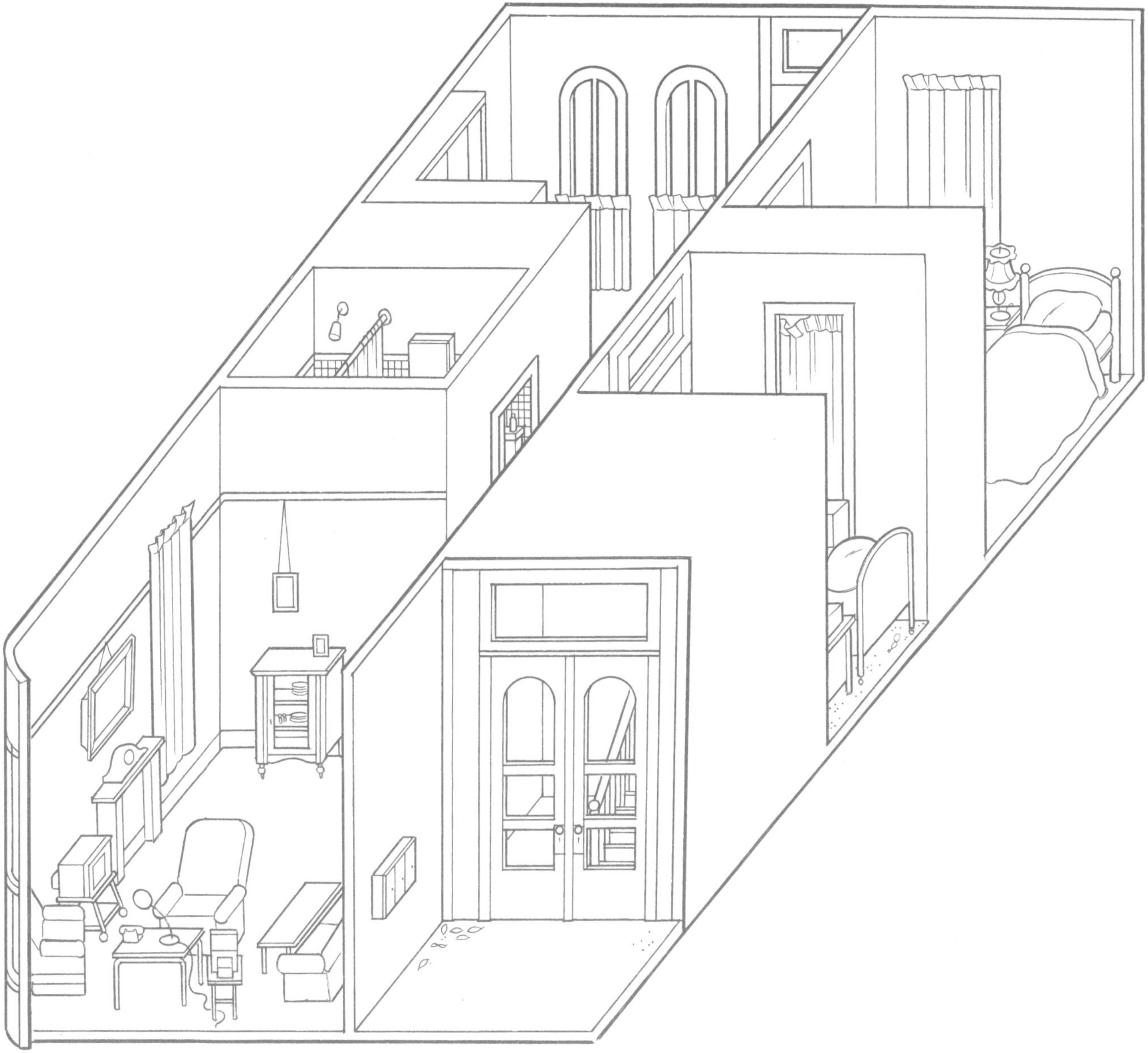

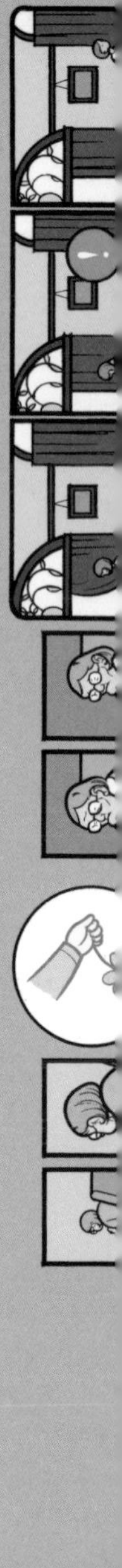

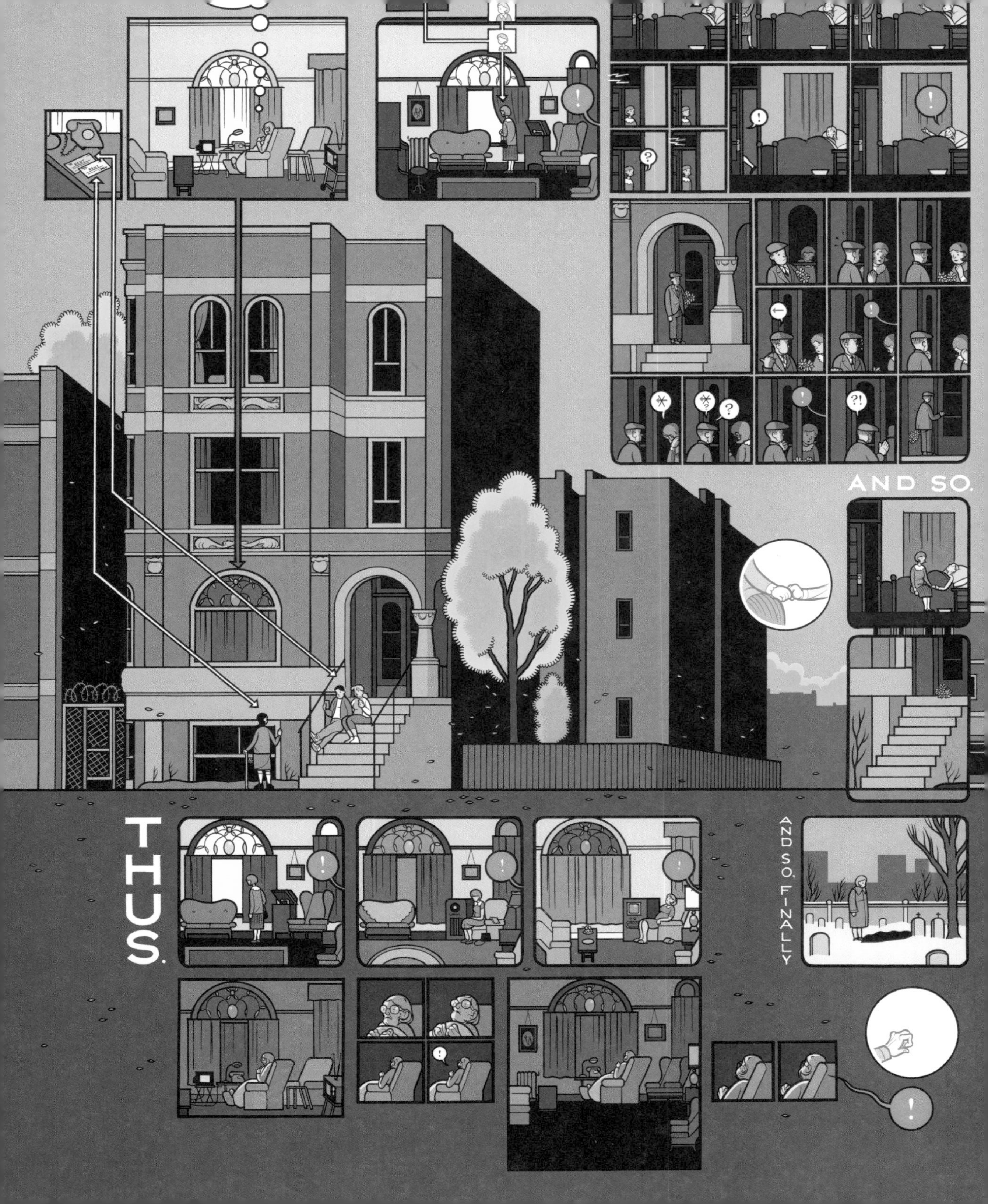
AND SO.
THUS.
AND SO, FINALLY

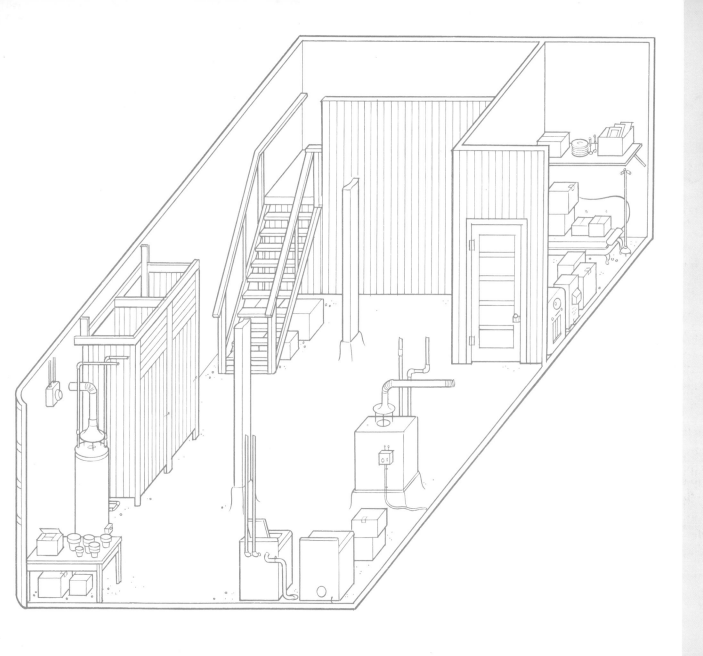